Math Wars

Math Wars

A Guide for Parents and Teachers

Carmen M. Latterell

Westport, Connecticut
London

Library of Congress Cataloging in Publication Data

Latterell, Carmen M.
    Math wars : a guide for parents and teachers / Carmen M. Latterell.
      p. cm.
    Includes bibliographical references and index.
    ISBN 0–275–98423–0 (alk. paper)
    1. Mathematics—Study and teaching—United States.   2. Parents—Education—
United States. I. Title.
    QA11.2.L37 2005
    510'.71'073—dc22   2004017652

British Library Cataloguing in Publication Data is available.

Library of Congress Catalog Card Number: 2004017652
ISBN: 0–275–98423–0

First published in 2005

Praeger Publishers, 88 Post Road West, Westport, CT 06881
An imprint of Greenwood Publishing Group, Inc.
www.praeger.com

Printed in the United States of America

The paper used in this book complies with the
Permanent Paper Standard issued by the National
Information Standards Organization (Z39.48–1984).

10 9 8 7 6 5 4 3 2 1

To Julius and Carol Latterell

Contents

Acknowledgments

Life is such a wonderful journey from one adventure to another, and writing this book has certainly been an adventure. I make my living teaching mathematics, a subject that I love. I also fear for the future of mathematics education and believe passionately that if mathematics education is to improve, it will take the intervention of parents. I was thrilled to write this book, as a step toward providing parents with the needed information, and that is why I am so overwhelmed with gratitude toward the people who made the book have life. I am predominately a mathematician, not a writer. I relied heavily on the generosity of Susan Slesinger, Executive Editor, Education, of Praeger Publishers. Susan believed in this book from the beginning. I cannot thank you enough, Susan.

A rather large group of parents, mathematics educators, and mathematicians read an early version of this book. Their subsequent comments and insights made the book much more balanced and accurate. I would like to single out one of them, a research mathematician from the University of Minnesota, Dr. Lawrence Gray. Dr. Gray was especially helpful with how it is that a mathematician thinks and feels, and what a mathematician values. Thank you, Larry. Of course, the mistakes remain mine, and there do remain areas in this book with which Dr. Gray will disagree.

As I wrote this book, it was natural to think about my own mathematics education. I imagine that readers might think about their mathematics education, as they read the book. In my own case, many good mathematics teachers had great influence on me. One stands out as extra special to me, Dr. Louis Friedler, currently a Professor of Mathematics at Arcadia University. Dr. Friedler was my first contact with a research mathematician, a college mathematics professor with a Ph.D. in mathematics. His clear love of mathematics, combined with his ability to both explain mathematics and encourage students, made an instant (and lasting) impression on me. It is fair to say that if Dr. Friedler had not entered my life, I would not be a mathematics professor today.

I also relied heavily on my parents, Julius and Carol Latterell, to whom I dedicate this book. My parents have devised a system of dividing their concerns. My father, who made his living teaching mathematics, read every chapter of the book several times before it entered the editing stage. His insights made this a much better book. My mother spent her time playing with my young child, Lily Marie Li. Lily had recently made the long trip from China to be my new daughter, and she needed lots of attention from caring adults. Someone once said this of my parents, "When you have a dream, your parents get right in there, shoulder to shoulder, and walk the path." Finally, to you little Lily, for making everything Mommy does have meaning.

CHAPTER 1

Introduction

Important issues are up for debate every day. If a reporter stopped you on the street and asked, what is the most important issue facing the United States today, what would you say? If you are a parent, you have many concerns for your children. You are worried about their safety, no doubt. Do you also worry about their education? Most parents do.

It is certainly true that among the important issues facing citizens of the United States *is* education. How best to educate our children seems to be up for continual debate. How much money should we spend on education? How are our children doing compared to those in the rest of the world? What is important to us? What do we want college graduates to know? Are enough of our citizens getting graduate degrees? Do we have enough scientists and are they smart enough? The issues and concerns go on and on.

Within all these concerns about education lie the concerns about mathematics education. When K–12 schools are asked to name their number one concern, they commonly name mathematics education. The United States continues to be very poor performing in worldwide competitions in K–12 students' mathematics test scores. Many K–12 students do not understand mathematics and do not like mathematics. Most students (and many adults) view mathematicians, and even students who are good in mathematics, as probably smart, but socially inept. Being good in mathematics is not something many students strive to be.

The solutions offered by mathematics education researchers are themselves up for debate. Are our students becoming too calculator dependent? Or should students be taking even more advantage of technology? Do students have basic arithmetic skills? If not, does it matter as long as students understand the concepts? If students are now learning more important content (such as statistics and discrete mathematics), is it then okay to let other skills fall by the wayside?

What if your child does not learn mathematics? How will he or she do on standardized tests? Will your daughter be able to major in whatever she chooses, or will mathematics be a stumbling block for her? Does your son know the mathematics that he needs to know to have a successful and happy life?

Are these questions really that important? Does mathematics education affect all of life, or even much of our lives? High school is always a time of turbulence. It sorts itself out in college, right? Actually, no, not in the case of mathematics. The issues about mathematics education go beyond K–12 grades.

Postsecondary mathematics courses are the fear of many students. Even among majors in mathematics there is now a disconnect between the teaching and learning (philosophically, pedagogically, and in content) of K–12 mathematics and postsecondary mathematics. The result is delays and difficulties in obtaining an undergraduate degree in mathematics. There is a national shortage of mathematics teachers, and many who are teaching were far from the nation's best mathematics students. Graduate programs in mathematics draw international students at a much higher rate than American students. Industries and government worry about the lack of mathematicians and scientists, and even the lack of mathematical knowledge among the majority of people. Everyone needs some mathematical knowledge. But, does everyone have that mathematical knowledge?

PARENTS

In the midst of all this are parents. Most parents have great anxiety and concern about mathematics education. In fact, the concerns parents have about mathematics education initiated the term "math wars." Although one might question the validity of going to "war" over mathematics education, there are many related issues that are extremely important. Parents *are* fearful that their children are not going to do well on standardized tests, and then will not have as many opportunities when applying for college. Parents *are* concerned that their children will not learn the basics of mathematics, and then will not function well as adults, or will not be able to succeed at the career they choose (even if the career is not mathematics-based). Many parents think their children are too dependent on calculators, and through that dependence, children are not learning how to do arithmetic.

However, what are parents to do? The current mathematics curriculum in many K–12 classrooms looks completely different from anything parents have experienced, even if they did well in mathematics. When parents see what children are bringing home, it is clear that their children are not working on the same mathematics parents remember from the time when they were in school. Besides lack of knowledge about mathematics education, many parents have an additional problem in that they feel they lack knowledge in mathematics itself. This is very intimidating; thus it is difficult for parents to do anything about the confusing state of mathematics education. And so, the cycle continues. If our children do not succeed in mathematics, will their children succeed? Probably not.

MATHEMATICS PROFESSORS

And, the situation is not much better for others. One might expect that mathematics professors, who clearly understand the 'mathematics' part of mathematics education, would have influence on mathematics education. In fact, one would hope that mathematics professors could take care of the issues in mathematics education and set everything right. In reality, most college mathematics professors are quite out of the loop when it comes to K–12 mathematics education. To understand this, we need to know that there is a very different program for people who end up calling themselves mathematicians or mathematics professors than for people who end up calling themselves mathematics educators.

Mathematics professors hold doctorates in mathematics. They have a specialty in some subcategory of mathematics. They likely have not taken a single course in education or mathematics education. They have some experience as graduate teaching assistants, and that has been viewed as enough 'education' on how to teach. Of course, it is not nearly enough, and most mathematics professors now recognize that fact. But, without training, mathematics professors tend to teach as they have been taught. And that is quite different from what is happening in the K–12 schools.

Many mathematics professors are not particularly good at teaching mathematics. Often when secondary teachers prove to be intelligent, but not good teachers, it is suggested that they become college mathematics teachers!

On the other hand, mathematics educators hold doctorates in mathematics education. Sometimes this degree is very separate from a mathematics department (and sometimes not). Often (and unfortunately it is quite often) mathematics educators lack master's degrees in mathematics. Only around 60 percent of doctorate programs in mathematics education require the equivalent of a master's degree in mathematics.[1] Although this certainly must change, it is the current situation.

So, we have mathematicians (holding doctorates in mathematics) and mathematics educators (holding doctorates in mathematics education) who are hardly on speaking terms. Besides the animosity between both sides, each side really does not know the needed language of the other side in order to communicate. Simply hoping that mathematicians and mathematics educators will get together and learn each other's language will not work for two reasons. First, there is a national shortage of mathematics educators. Second, most mathematics educators take positions in education departments, which are separate from mathematics departments.

Despite the difficulties of bridging the gap, mathematics professors are hungry for information about mathematics education. In fact, they desire information as much as parents do, although for different reasons. Mathematics professors want to be better at teaching. They want to apply for National Science Foundation grants that call for some knowledge about mathematics education. Mathematics professors are concerned about the direction that K–12 mathematics education appears to be taking, and they want to contribute toward a different direction. However, lack of knowledge about the field of mathematics education prevents contribution. Even lack of knowledge of the jargon in the field of mathematics education holds mathematicians back from fully contributing.

ELEMENTARY AND SECONDARY MATHEMATICS TEACHERS

If parents and mathematics professors are not determining the direction of mathematics education, then who is? A good guess might be the elementary and secondary mathematics teachers. After all, they are the teachers!

Actually, elementary teachers have even less of a chance than mathematics professors of influencing the field of mathematics education. Elementary teachers are called on to be specialists in all areas, including mathematics, but often suffer from an insufficient background in mathematics. Usually they are expected to teach mathematics without having either much experience in mathematics or mathematics education. Lately, elementary teachers are handed a mathematics curriculum based on the National Council of Teachers of Mathematics principles and told to teach it. This curriculum is completely different from any they have ever seen before, and not only do they lack the mathematics background to teach it successfully, they do not have the education background to do so.

Secondary mathematics teachers are only a little better off. Many of them have the equivalent of a bachelor's degree in mathematics, some mathematics education courses, and many general education courses. However, almost none of them has a background in mathematics education research, and thus they are likely not doing the decision-making. In fact, many secondary mathematics teachers are caught up in the math wars themselves; not happy with the very curriculum they are being told to teach and not feeling they have a voice. Secondary mathematics teachers are feeling pressure from many sides. They must meet state standards, produce students who have excellent scores on standardized tests, and, in general, keep everyone happy. Keeping everyone happy is nearly impossible, because various agents want nearly opposite things. Even to say that everyone wants a mathematically literate population is not helpful. The very definition of mathematical literacy differs. I might think someone is mathematically literate if he or she can do arithmetic calculations and solve day-to-day mathematical problems. Someone else might define mathematical literacy as being able to use a calculator to problem-solve and to make decisions about mathematical situations that arise in life. These may appear to be similar descriptions, but they are quite different. By the end of this book, you will understand the depth of the differences. Out of frustration, some mathematics teachers leave the classroom and pursue doctorates so that they might have more influence on mathematics education. However, rarely do they return to secondary teaching. Even if they try to return to secondary teaching, most school districts do not hire people with doctorates (their salaries would be too high).

OTHER STAKEHOLDERS

Besides parents, mathematics professors, and K–12 teachers, there are other stakeholders who do not have a voice. Science educators and science professors are very concerned about the state of mathematics education. It is difficult to teach chemistry to students who do not know how to solve an algebraic equation. Business, industry, and government all have a stake in mathematics education.

I cannot tell you how many times I have been overcharged at a store, and tried to explain the mathematics of what they are doing wrong (so they can do it differently) to clerks who have no concept of what I am explaining. Not only is it disturbing to think about clerks' lack of knowledge, but what does a customer do who does not understand mathematics? I imagine, many customers simply pay the wrong charge, not only because of an inability to explain how to do it correctly, but because the customer is not mathematical enough to realize he or she is being overcharged in the first place.

This brings me to the statement that students have a huge stake in mathematics education! They have a huge stake for all the reasons that I have mentioned up to this point. Even if they are never parents, mathematics teachers, or do anything related to mathematics, mathematics is a part of everyday life. But, none of these people I have named (including, and especially, students) is in a position to do something about the issues surrounding mathematics education.

THE NATIONAL COUNCIL OF TEACHERS OF MATHEMATICS

Perhaps it is time in this discussion to pause for a moment to understand who does have a voice. The strongest voice in K–12 mathematics education is the National Council of Teachers of Mathematics (NCTM). It is a powerful organization that has written sets of standards for K–12 mathematics, and much of the current mathematics curricula call themselves NCTM-oriented. Just what NCTM is will be explained in this book, but suffice to say at the moment, NCTM does not include many of the stakeholders (or at least not in sufficient number to matter).

Very few parents or mathematics professors are in NCTM, although some elementary teachers and many secondary mathematics teachers are members. However, the majority of secondary mathematics teachers across the United States do not involve themselves in the decision-making or policy-setting. The majority of secondary mathematics teachers are not involved with NCTM to any significant degree, if for no other reason than because they are too busy teaching to involve themselves in organizational activities. Most secondary mathematics teachers do not read the research journal that NCTM publishes. As mentioned, most secondary teachers do not research in mathematics education. They do not have the time, or the background, to do so. Although it is true that NCTM membership includes many secondary mathematics teachers, it is not true that most secondary mathematics teachers are actively involved with NCTM. Most are not.

The strongest voices in NCTM are those of mathematics educators (people with doctorates in mathematics education). Mathematics educators, through NCTM, have the voices in mathematics education. I believe that it is a huge mistake to have only one type of thinker in charge of anything. The results of having mathematics educators as the only strong voice in mathematics education include a situation known as the math wars, and a lopsided view of mathematics education. The math wars is a term used for the debates about mathematics education. The two sides of the debates are those who want mathematics curriculum in alignment with the NCTM, and those who do not. This is not to suggest that the math wars are caused by NCTM, as such. Indeed, NCTM would like everyone to support them, and then there would be no need for the math wars. And in fact, I have often heard the math wars "blamed" on the other side for this reason (i.e., if there were no disagreement, there would be no debate). However, I believe the intensity of the debate occurs because one side (predominately mathematics educators through NCTM) is making the decisions about mathematics education for all stakeholders. Every situation in life needs checks and balances, and no one wants all decisions about something that is very important to be made by others, even if those others are experts. But we are currently in a situation where it is difficult for others to speak up, because they do not know enough about mathematics education to feel comfortable with speaking.

THIS BOOK

It is the objective of this book to empower anyone who has an interest in mathematics education, but who lacks the necessary background and information on mathematics education to make a difference. This book will offer tools to enable parents, mathematics teachers, mathematics professors, and others to know what is going on and to be able to react as they want to react. This book will be useful for seminars for graduate teaching assistants in mathematics in addition to graduate students at the master's level in mathematics education, who will find it to be a useful survey of their field. Given the importance of the topic of mathematics education, professionals in other areas of academics (science education, science content areas) as well as individuals outside of academe will be able to make good use of the information in this book.

Of all these stakeholders, however, this book is designed to speak directly and from the heart to parents. It is time that parents have the needed tools to have a say in the mathematical education of their children. The main goal of this book is to open a window into the field of mathematics education through which parents can look. By the end of this book, parents will know what they want to say.

Each chapter in this book is self-contained. With the exception of beginning with some history of mathematics education and ending with further resources, the order of the chapters is somewhat arbitrary. Except for the most rudimentary of knowledge about mathematics education, no assumptions regarding reader background have been made. The book is accessible to all who have an interest and want to have a voice in mathematics education.

Although I have definite opinions about the math wars, and it may even become clear through the reading of this book on which side I fall, I have taken great pains in writing this book to present a balanced view. I want the reader to be free to view all positions on the math wars in a "tell it like it is" style. The reader will then be left with the knowledge necessary to form a view of his or her own.

As a parent, you might have heard of the debates over "whole language" in reading. Research supported whole language. Many parents did not like whole language and felt that their children were not learning to read. Even though the debates roared for a long time, they were eventually resolved. Just as parents care that their children can read, parents also care that their children can do mathematics. Much like the debates over whole language in reading, the math wars will subside when everyone is able to participate. When all voices have been heard, I predict that the math wars will no longer have the power to continue. But, all voices will not be heard until all people (including parents) are speaking. You are invited, then, to empower yourself with this short course in the math wars.

A GREATLY SIMPLIFIED PICTURE OF THE SUBJECT

In order to understand the chapters to come and facilitate your ability to read chapters in whatever order desired, a small amount of information needs to be presented up front. The following paragraph, which greatly oversimplifies the situation in mathematics education, is necessary to ease your burden.

The National Council of Teachers of Mathematics (NCTM) has written and disseminated two sets of standards (the second is a revision of the first). Most mathematics educators (people who do research in mathematics education) believe that NCTM is correct with their standards. Most current mathematics curricula are written to support the standards; I will call them NCTM-oriented. Quite a few (but not all) mathematicians and parents, and other stakeholders, believe that NCTM is mistaken about several issues; they think that the NCTM-oriented curriculum is not a good approach and they want mathematics education to return to the more traditional curriculum. Thus, the math wars debate: those in favor of NCTM and those against.

I caution you that great simplifications have been made in the preceding paragraph, but I promise you that by the end of the book, the simplifications will be expanded with fuller explanations. For now, it is important that you have some sense of the situation. Throughout the course of this book, various terms and jargon will be defined. However, we need a small set of terms to begin the process. A larger glossary can be found at the end of the book.

TERMS

Mathematician: One who holds an advanced degree (probably a Ph.D.) in mathematics and works in industry, government, or teaching.

Mathematics education: The formal teaching and learning of mathematics at any level (kindergarten through postgraduate).

Mathematics education as a major: One who majors in mathematics education and studies both mathematics (although usually not in as much depth as needed) and education. A person holding a Ph.D. in mathematics education conducts research in the teaching and learning of mathematics.

Mathematics educator: One who holds an advanced degree (probably a Ph.D.) in mathematics education and works mostly in either a mathematics department or an education department (this is more likely) at a college or university. Some work for the government (such as for the National Science Foundation or in state education departments).

Mathematics professor: One who holds an advanced degree (probably a Ph.D.) in mathematics and works at a college or university. Thus, mathematics professors are mathematicians, but not all mathematicians are mathematics professors. Further, mathematics professors usually have a position that includes three main components: research, teaching, and service. Depending on the institution, some of these components are more valued than others, with the usual order of importance the one given. Professional service includes such activities as committee work and reviewing articles. Thus, although mathematics professors teach mathematics, the teaching of mathematics is not always the largest or most important part of their positions.

Mathematics teacher: One who teaches mathematics at the secondary level (roughly seventh through twelfth grades). (Most elementary teachers also teach some mathematics, but they call themselves elementary teachers, not mathematics teachers.)

NCTM: The National Council of Teachers of Mathematics is a powerful organization. The vast, vast majority of mathematics educators follow and believe in the precepts of the NCTM.

NCTM-oriented: Curricula (or philosophies) that are based on the standards and principles of the National Council of Teachers of Mathematics.

Traditional: Curricula (or philosophies) that are *not* based on the standards and principles of the National Council of Teachers of Mathematics, and might differ from those principles in substantial ways. For example, traditional mathematics curricula are much less calculator-dependent than NCTM-oriented curricula.

SUMMARY

Mathematics education is in crisis. Secondary students are not learning basic mathematics, not achieving well on standardized tests, and not entering college prepared for mathematical fields. This book explains the issues surrounding the heated debates, called the math wars, about mathematics education. The math wars have two sides: the side favoring curricula in alignment with the National Council of Teachers of Mathematics (NCTM) standards and philosophy, and the side, called traditional, which would rather return to how mathematics was taught before NCTM's standards. Most mathematics educators (people with doctorates in mathematics education) support the NCTM-oriented side, but many mathematicians (people with doctorates in mathematics) support the traditional side. Most parents and mathematics teachers do not have enough knowledge about the issues to support either side. This book presents both sides of the math wars in a fair and balanced manner. Stakeholders in mathematics education, who have not had a voice, will gain the information that is needed in order to be heard.

CHAPTER 2

What Preceded the Math Wars?

We need to consider the past in order to learn from it. Unfortunately, when it comes to mathematics education, history will reveal that the United States has not learned from the past. It is not important that the reader remember particular dates, people, documents, or places in mathematics education history. Rather, it is crucial that you come to understand what I will call the great pendulum swing. Think of a good, fully wound grandfather clock with a huge pendulum that swings steadily from side to side. The pendulum does not slow down in its swing in order to come slowly to a stop in the middle. It does not find a balance. One keeps a clock wound to avoid just such a thing and to keep the pendulum in continual movement. The history will show that with regard to mathematics education, our nation has behaved like a good, fully wound grandfather clock.

Unfortunately, what is good in a clock is not good for mathematics education! However, the nation seems to take steps to wind the clock so that the pendulum never finds a balance. The current math wars can be visualized as the National Council of Teachers of Mathematics (NCTM) at one end of the pendulum swing (call this end NCTM-oriented), holding on so that it does not swing to the other side. At the other side are mathematicians who hope and predict that the pendulum will swing back again to their end (call this side traditional). The NCTM will argue that the pendulum will not swing back to traditional because of the effort and research that has gone into the current curricula. Of course, people who are hoping that the pendulum does swing back to the traditional end do not put much stock in that argument. (By the way, some mathematicians do support NCTM and some mathematics educators do not support NCTM. Do not infer that all mathematicians are on one side of the math wars and all mathematics educators are on the other side. In general, however, mathematicians are more likely to be opposed to NCTM, and mathematics educators are much more likely to be in favor of NCTM.)

One more word about the term "traditional": I could actually use the term "traditional" for the side labeled NCTM. There is no "tradition" (in the long term) in mathematics education. The history of mathematics education will reveal times that curricula opposite of NCTM-oriented were in place and times when NCTM-like curricula were in place. There might not have been an NCTM organization at that time, but there were two types of curricula that kept coming into fashion: one that I will call traditional and one that I will call NCTM-oriented, in keeping with current parlance. To understand the math wars, we must know enough of the history of mathematics education to understand the great pendulum swing between these two approximate curricula types. In sum, mathematics education has swung between two sides throughout history. Currently the two sides, NCTM-oriented and traditional (or non-NCTM-oriented), compose the math wars.

A FEW ARGUMENTS

Before we begin the history, it is appropriate that we examine a few more arguments that call upon history for their evidence. Sometimes people who are in favor of the NCTM-oriented point of view will argue that nothing up to this point in mathematics education has been very successful, and so we might as well try something new. Of course, NCTM-oriented is then presented as the "something new." Mathematics education history is actually not abundant in success. However, the argument is also weak in that it is more of an argument against something (traditional) than for something (NCTM-oriented). How do we know that the NCTM-oriented approach works, either? Maybe we have swung from bad to bad. And why isn't it better to fix what is wrong with what we have rather than throw it out and try something new? Thus, the argument (on either side), that "because there is not a history of success in mathematics education, we should _____ [fill in the blank]," is very unconvincing.

Another argument, which surprisingly is used both for and against the NCTM-oriented point of view, is that the history of mathematics education shows we have never stayed with anything long enough to truly determine if the curriculum is good or not. History reveals that, at about the time something starts to work, the pendulum has swung in the other direction. But, this argument is used both to say "return to traditional and give it time" and also to say "stay with NCTM-oriented and give it time." This argument as well is not terribly convincing for either side: that is, if traditional was no good, why return to it? And if NCTM-oriented is not good, then is staying with it longer just stretching out something that is not good? A curriculum must be supported on its merits, and not by pitting it against other curricula and arguing for more time. Our children should not be guinea pigs for mathematics curricula. There ought to be a better way to make decisions.

WHAT DO WE MEAN BY HISTORY?

Some basic knowledge of the history of mathematics education will help us in our attempt to understand the current state in mathematics education. Extensive writing exists regarding the history of mathematics education. The purpose of this chapter is to give an overview only. This chapter concentrates on history only within the United States. The purpose of providing this history is to allow you, as stakeholders, to understand and influence mathematics education in the United States.

The history of interest to us is that of mathematics education. It is necessary to know at least some of the "when, where, how, and who" in mathematics teaching and learning. This book addresses mostly kindergarten through twelfth-grade education, but this book will also touch on postsecondary mathematics teaching and learning to help set the scene.

This book is not involved with the history of mathematics. Of course, that is a fascinating history as well, but it is not important for understanding the math wars. However, you will notice that how one defines mathematics tends to change throughout the history of mathematics education. Because of this, I have not yet attempted to define mathematics. As soon as we begin the history, however, we will need to define mathematics.

THE BEGINNING AND A DEFINITION OF MATHEMATICS

A beginning point for describing the history of K–12 mathematics education could be before the formation of schools. But since this book is offering a brief history, let us move quickly to the first schools. Reading and writing were the chief goals, and writing probably did include writing numbers and counting. Arithmetic textbooks were soon to follow. Teachers probably had very little mathematics ability themselves. A lesson most likely consisted of the teacher giving an arithmetic rule (perhaps how to add two-digit numbers by two-digit numbers), showing a few examples, and then leaving students left to work out exercises on their own. The first colleges tended not to require (nor actually offer) mathematics courses.

People who have little true experience with mathematics often think that mathematics is arithmetic. And that is what mathematics was at this point in history, as far as the schools were concerned. Perhaps a definition of arithmetic will help. Basic arithmetic might include the addition, subtraction, multiplication, and division of whole numbers. More advanced arithmetic might include these same operations of rational numbers (this will include fractions and decimals).

Arithmetic is actually a part of mathematics. However, arithmetic is not all there is to mathematics. Mathematics also includes algebra, geometry, real analysis, complex analysis, number theory, combinatorics, probability theory, statistics, topology, and many other areas. It is not important that you know what those areas are, but only that mathematics includes many topics besides arithmetic. Even so, some mathematicians define mathematics not in terms of any of these areas, but they try to describe what mathematics is to them.

The following are definitions of mathematics. Notice that they differ, which may seem bizarre, but there is no firm agreement on just what mathematics is. Definitions of mathematics include the following:

- A foreign language
- Symbols and the methods for manipulating symbols
- A science of patterns
- Reasoning and logic
- Everything (This means that mathematics is found in nature, and that the world is mathematical. Mathematics then is a possible framework for understanding the world.)

- A practical tool, made up of procedures needed in life, which is largely quantitative
- An art: it is about beauty

If you are confused, take heart. At three different points in the semester, I assign a paper to my students in a particular undergraduate junior-level mathematics course. I tell them to answer the question: What is mathematics? My students struggle with this assignment, and they answer the question very differently. Their *own* definitions change during the course of the semester, and I take this as evidence that I am doing my job. (Appendix 2 gives more information about defining mathematics.) Let us leave it at this for now: at the time when schools were forming, arithmetic and mathematics were one in the same as far as mathematics education was concerned. The pendulum was at its beginning, and it sat on the side of basic skills (the traditional side).

In the 1800s, arithmetic settled into the early grades, and secondary schools took up the topics of algebra and geometry. Colleges began to require some mathematics. It was in the 1800s that teachers began undergoing training in the normal schools. The teaching of mathematics became quite formal (full of symbols, for example). Educators viewed the brain as a muscle, and mathematics as exercise that could strengthen this muscle. This point of view is not popular today among mathematics educators, but some mathematicians still like this view.

The traditional curricula of the 1800s are not even remotely the same as today's NCTM-oriented. This time in history was one in which pure mathematics won out (mathematics for mathematics' sake). Although different from basic skills, the curricula of the 1800s were also different from our current curricula. Perhaps the best way to think about the curricula of the 1800s is that the pendulum began on the side of mathematicians, and then the pendulum swung even further in that same direction. The pendulum did not come toward the middle, but swung further out. And so the definition simply widens to include more than arithmetic. With the next piece of history, the pendulum swings in the opposite direction.

AN OPPOSITE SWING

Toward the end of the 1800s and the beginning of the 1900s, the practical needs of society took over. The pendulum went past the middle and moved to the other end. The argument that mathematics is studied to strengthen the brain was rejected. Mathematics was studied for its direct practical applications or not studied at all. Arithmetic was the topic for the youngest children, and the junior and senior high schools included not just algebra and geometry, but statistics, trigonometry, and work with functions (that is, a mapping or association between objects in two sets according to some rule; in addition, it has to be the case that for every object in the first set, only one element can be paired in the second set).

Interestingly enough, it was at this time that the first doctorates in mathematics education were awarded. People who have doctorates in mathematics education are almost without exception NCTM-oriented. So, as the pendulum swung, the mathematics educators were first being educated. Both the setting up of a national school system and the increased concern about teacher education contributed to mathematics education emerging as a field of its own. Mathematics education is intended to be a mixture of graduate-level mathematics and graduate-level education. But one could not reasonably create this major by requiring a full major in *both* of these fields; rather, doctorates in mathematics education took a subset of each. The teaching and learning of mathematics is quite distinct from the teaching and learning of any other academic subject. To separate doctorates in mathematics education into its own degree is reasonable.

We will not continue to trace the history of doctorates in mathematics education, because, frankly, it does not impact our topic. And yet, mathematics educators are very influential in the math wars. Still, for as much power as they have, it is interesting that the major remains unpopular. As of the writing of this chapter, there is a nationwide shortage of people with doctorates in mathematics education. In 2000–2001, 49 percent of all positions advertised for mathematics education went unfilled. In 1990 through 1999, only from 80 to 115 people received doctorates in mathematics education annually.[1]

PROGRESSIVE EDUCATION

From around 1920 up to 1950, the best description of mathematics education is to call it "progressive education." The nature of the child (with John Dewey as a spokesman) won out, with curriculum becoming very child-centered. Although the pendulum swung, it did not swing back to the middle. Rather the pendulum swung much, much further in line with NCTM-oriented curricula.

Here is an illustration of the pendulum swing in mathematics education. In the line segment below, C is the middle, the balance spot. In all of the history of mathematics education, and through today, the pendulum has not stopped at the point of balance. Let us call point A the traditional spot, and point E the NCTM-oriented spot. Although the past has been neither exactly traditional nor exactly NCTM-oriented, the spots at which the pendulum has paused have been very similar. So, from the time schools began until this point in our discussion, the pendulum has done this: began at B, swung to A, swung to D, and then swung to E. We are at spot E in our discussion. Again, the curriculum is not exactly an NCTM-oriented curriculum, but it has a lot in common with NCTM-oriented issues and ideas.

A	B	C	D	E
	Traditional Side	Balance	NCTM Side	

One of the reasons I believe it is important to study history in order to discuss the current state of mathematics education is to realize that mathematics education has never stopped at point C. In some opinions, the perfect side is neither side, but it is point C. Most people from both sides of the math wars would at least pay lip service to the opinion that the perfect side is neither side, but it is point C. But I believe, in all honesty, that most people have a preference for one side or the other. Some argue that the math wars will end when we do reach point C. But, I personally believe that the next step will be to swing back to traditional. In other words, I am fearful that the pendulum will continue to swing back and forth for some time yet. Alas, I am getting ahead of the story.

Let us return to 1920 through 1950, and we are sitting around point E. Mathematics education took on a slow pace, with discovery learning a popular pedagogy. Discovery learning is not easy to explain. Roughly, the idea is that students will remember what they discover for themselves, and not what they have been told. So the teacher, instead of explaining a rule, might set up a mathematical experiment, the goal of which is for the students to discover the rule. Since it might be difficult for you to envision a mathematical experiment, let me give an example.

Here is a trigonometric function: $f(x) = A\sin(x)$. It is not important if this function means very much to you, but notice the A. The A is a parameter, and if I enter different values (numbers) for A, the graph of the function will change. The parameter A has an effect on the graph. And as one might expect in mathematics, the effect is predictable. The teacher could simply tell the students what changes in A will do (for example, as A gets larger, the graph stretches in height). Or (as in discovery learning), the teacher could show the students various graphs for different values of A. With today's graphing calculators, the students could provide these graphs for themselves. The teacher could ask the students to predict what will happen if the value of A changes again. In this manner, the student will discover the rule for the parameter A.

Unfortunately, what tended to happen during this period of history was that the teachers were inexperienced and went overboard with discovery learning. They did not provide enough guidance. The children set the pace of instruction and sometimes even selected the topics.

Another interesting note about the progressive education period is the formation of NCTM in 1920. An organization of mathematics professors, called the Mathematical Association of America, already existed at that time. Ironically, the Mathematical Association of America was to a significant degree responsible for forming NCTM; "ironically" because today many of the members of the two organizations are on opposite sides of the math wars. Although NCTM formed in 1920, it did not become powerful until sixty years later, in 1980.

In the last ten years of the progressive education period, a time of great frustration took over. Many plans had been put in place, and yet it was becoming increasingly clear that educated people had very little training in mathematics. For example, the army began teaching arithmetic to recruits, because the recruits did not have basic arithmetic skills. At this same time, some citizens of our nation had excelled in scientific (and engineering) discoveries. Clearly, mathematics is important, and some of the population was able to use mathematics to improve everybody's lives. It became a large concern that if so many children were growing up unable to do mathematics, then this excelling in scientific discoveries would come to an end. The discovery learning (or letting the child rule) did not seem to be working. So the response was to let that old pendulum swing.

NEW MATH

The next period is called the time of "New Math." New Math began in the 1950s and lasted until 1971. The pendulum swing into New Math was a very wide arc, all the way back to around point A. By and large, mathematicians were in charge of the New Math movement. In that sense, New Math is closer to traditional curricula than NCTM-oriented. However, New Math was not exactly traditional curricula. In fact, rote learning got a bad name and basic skills suffered. It is because of this last fact that sometimes people think New Math is more like NCTM-oriented curricula than it is like traditional curricula. In fact, when someone wants to criticize NCTM-oriented curricula, they call it New New Math. This is a large criticism because New Math did not work well. It is important to understand, however, that New Math and NCTM-oriented curricula really have nothing to do with each other. The NCTM-oriented curricula are NOT an updated version of New Math.

New Math can be explained as follows. Although mathematical procedures were taught, they were taught in terms of logical explanations. The use of set theory even in the early grades became popular. The mathematics was taught in a very abstract manner. Applications were virtually absent from New Math curricula. And if the curriculum did occasionally include a word problem, the setting was something very adult, not something to which a child could relate. Little ones were very confused! Symbolism was used for everything, even for solving problems that required no symbolism. Technical language was pushed. Let me give an example: when learning algebra, we tell students to solve for x. In New Math algebra, we told students to solve for a variable over a domain ... blah, blah, technical, technical, math term, math term, etc., ad nauseam. And it made as much sense as that last sentence made to you. Formal language was emphasized beyond what a K–12 student could possibly understand or care about.

Imagine if your young child asked you about "the birds and the bees." If you answered your little one with a biology lecture worthy of a Ph.D. in biology, you would have the equivalent of New Math. Is it important that you answer your child correctly? Yes. But, it is not important that you give details to such a degree that the child becomes hopelessly confused. In fact, it is not only not important, it is inappropriate. New Math was inappropriate.

Bruner was a spokesman well known in the education world, and he believed that you could teach any major concept to anyone, at any age, as long as you broke it into little pieces. Along with all the other issues, New Math introduced the so-called "spiral" in mathematics curriculum; that is, the idea that one should teach each mathematical topic lightly and return to it every year. At a much later time, some people became fond of saying that mathematics textbooks were a mile wide (included so many different topics) but an inch thick (the topics were never covered in any kind of depth).[2] The best way to describe New Math is that it was set theory for everyone, including kindergartners.

By the way, New Math was studied by researchers and declared a good idea, a success. Here is why: teachers were given lots of money and graduate credits for studying the New Math curricula and trying it out. The best students were given to these teachers. Big shock! It all worked out well. Dear parent, remember to ALWAYS take research with a grain of salt.

New Math may have died earlier had it not been for *Sputnik* (the first space satellite). *Sputnik* was sent into space in 1957 by the Soviet Union. They not only sent *Sputnik* into orbit, but they figuratively sent the United States into orbit as well. *Sputnik* was treated as a major embarrassment to the country. How could the Soviet Union accomplish what we could not? The only "logical" response was that our education system was not teaching mathematics or science well enough. Who better to fix it than mathematicians?

Calling New Math a disaster is a bit harsh—only a bit. There were many reasons that New Math just would not work. Spiraling curriculum had a bad effect on slower kids, as spiraling curriculum ignored the abstraction level that children could handle. Technical vocabulary was pushed too early, as was symbolism. The role of problem-solving was reduced to being only an application. Many secondary teachers could not themselves handle the mathematics involved, let alone teach it.

Having mathematicians without mathematics educators in charge of mathematics education was clearly not the answer. Mathematicians do not have enough education background to be in charge. (Note that during New Math, many K–12 mathematics teachers were advising the mathematicians. However, mathematics educators [people with doctorates in mathematics education] were not advising.) On the other hand, having mathematics educators without mathematicians in charge of mathematics education is not the answer, either. Mathematics educators do not have enough mathematics background to be in charge.

Today the mathematics educators are in charge, but certainly claim that they are involving mathematicians. There is a set of mathematicians on advisory boards for the NCTM-oriented curricula. However, that is very different from a true partnership between mathematicians and mathematics educators. The mathematicians are not joint authors on the NCTM-oriented curricula, for example. So, during the New Math era, the mathematicians were in charge, and today, during NCTM-oriented times, the mathematics educators are in charge. This secondary pendulum within the primary pendulum is just as destructive, because both types of people must be involved.[3]

MATH ANXIETY

Let's take a break from history and talk about math anxiety. The reason for raising the topic of math anxiety at this point in this book is that, it is possible that you suffered or suffer from math anxiety, and that that suffering was a direct cause of New Math.

First, what is math anxiety? Well, it is a terror of mathematics. I do not have math anxiety. But, I have public speaking anxiety. You know that feeling when you have to do something that you don't want to do? You sweat. You feel sick to your stomach. Maybe your hands shake. Your face is red. You might lie awake in bed the night before, dreading what you have to do. All of that happens to me when I must speak in public. And I think that is a common problem. Some people fear mathematics the way most of us fear public speaking. Actually, millions of people suffer from math anxiety. Around the time of New Math, approximately one-third of all students had math anxiety.

Let me borrow two sentences from one of many books I own on math anxiety: "Not unlike a disease, math anxiety . . . is a clear-cut, negative, mental, emotional, and/or physical reaction to mathematical thought processes and problem solving. It is often caused by negative experiences with math in childhood or early adolescence."[4]

Another book defines math anxiety as math *panic*. I think math panic is a better term than math anxiety. It is more descriptive. It is more accurate. Because I teach mathematics, math anxiety is an important topic for me. Another current book (*Math: Facing an American Phobia*) clearly defines math anxiety as math phobia and claims that two-thirds of all Americans have math phobia. (The author also ranks math phobia up there with public speaking, as I did, and also with fear of heights and snakes!)[5]

So, math anxiety is an intense fear of mathematics, and the fear prevents the person from being able to do mathematics. If your child has math anxiety, it will prevent him from learning mathematics.

The idea is that some methods and periods of time in mathematics education (such as the New Math era) were notorious for creating math anxiety in people. There is no question that NCTM-oriented curricula are less likely to create math anxiety in students than New Math was. And, NCTM-oriented curricula are probably less likely to create math anxiety in students than traditional mathematics curricula are. This is something you should think about when deciding on which side of the math wars you are.

Here is a quick explanation why NCTM-oriented curricula are not likely to create math anxiety in students. Students are capable of thinking, and NCTM-oriented curricula are about thinking. The NCTM-oriented curricula use various pedagogies (including group work) that appeal to a variety of students and reduce anxiety. NCTM-oriented curricula are light on drill and rote learning, which also reduces math anxiety. Brain researchers (and psychologists) know that different areas of the brain are used for different mathematical tasks. Some mathematical tasks are easier than others. Retrieving math facts is the biggest problem for elementary students, and thus if this is deemphasized, so is math anxiety. Another reason that NCTM-oriented curricula tend to produce less math anxiety than traditional curricula is that anxiety gets produced when one is not successful at something. More students are successful at NCTM-oriented curricula than are successful at traditional curricula. Gaining success builds confidence and reduces anxiety. In fact, the best method for overcoming math anxiety is to find some method of having a little success in mathematics. Very few students were successful in New Math, and therefore math anxiety rose.

BACK TO THE BASICS

Returning to our story, by 1971, New Math was "officially" over, having been dropped by authorities with amazing speed as it was realized that New Math was not working. (So much for the research that supported it.

Remember this when you hear arguments about research support of NCTM-oriented curricula and about using research support as the sole determining factor about what curriculum to use.) However, school districts that had spent money on textbooks continued to use the New Math textbooks into the 1970s while mathematics education had washed its hands of the mess. This is a good example of how removed the actual teaching and learning of mathematics is from the field of mathematics education. I know this is difficult to comprehend, but schools are usually the last to "catch up."

From 1971 to 1975, no particular theme held throughout mathematics education. Mathematics educators believed with greater fervor that Piaget was in fact correct, but this did not materialize into a particular result. Piaget said that children follow a pattern of development, and there is no point trying to teach adult-level mathematical reasoning to a kindergartner, no matter how small you break up the pieces. This four-year period does not fit the pendulum map. Rather, one curriculum fad after another occurred.

By 1975 the fads had settled into one cry: "Let's go back to the basics!" Ah, that pendulum swung. This is best thought of as remaining on the same side, but swinging toward the middle. In other words, we are at point B. Let's review the entire history again: when schools began, we were at Point B, then we swung to A, and then a radical swing to D. After D, there was a small swing to E, and then another radical swing, landing at A, and now back to B. It is not important that you remember this pattern. It is only important that you understand that the pendulum is constantly in motion.

A	B	C	D	E
	Traditional Side	Balance	NCTM Side	

At this point in time, rote learning was stressed, with drill, drill, drill, and yes, even more drill. Mathematics was no longer about symbolism, and "cookbook" mathematics was born (that is, mathematical procedures were taught, which were broken into little steps, and the resulting "recipe" was told to the students). Very little thought was expected of students. Although it may appear that the pendulum did not swing far, let us consider a separate pendulum. Think of one side being New Math and the other being Back To the Basics. New Math had too much emphasis on symbolism. Back To the Basics had nearly no emphasis on symbolism. Symbolism is important in mathematics, but it is not everything in mathematics. Yet, there is no balancing point on this issue. An interesting dissertation could examine why the middle ground is never found. Actually, I think the Nobel Prize could be awarded to whomever solves that conundrum.

THE TIME OF PROBLEM-SOLVING

The period from 1979 to 1989 could best be labeled the time of problem-solving. Yes, the pendulum swung again. This is probably point D. And of course, the idea was that Back To the Basics was, well, too basic. Forget about the basics, and concentrate on solving word problems. The NCTM exerted some power during that time.

At the beginning of 1980, NCTM published *An Agenda for Action*.[6] In that document, it was advised that problem-solving ought to be at the center of K–12 mathematics. Basic skills were downplayed. The belief was that calculators could replace basic skills; and, the learning of problem-solving strategies was much more important, because a calculator could not replace the learning of problem-solving. Also, NCTM believed that if students learned problem-solving, they would be more inclined to go back and pick up the basic skills. Although *An Agenda for Action* was dwarfed by another document that NCTM did not author, it still was the case that mathematics curricula were full of problem-solving. I suppose the best way to think of this was that word problems took over. Take note once again, reader. The very issue that had previously been at the core (basic skills) was now being viewed as unimportant. When that old pendulum decides to swing, it swings with a vengeance!

In 1983, *A Nation at Risk* was published by T. H. Bell, secretary of education at the time.[7] Knowing the title and that it is about mathematics education (actually the report was also about other school subjects), one might be able to guess the contents. In sum, *A Nation at Risk* did proclaim that the United States was at risk because few knew how to do mathematics. A famous line is worth repeating. "Our nation is at risk ... the educational foundations of our society are presently being eroded by a rising tide of mediocrity that threatens our very future as a nation and a people."[8] Certainly, the report did not lie with regard to the statistics on the number of poor scores on standardized mathematics tests, and the number of people in remedial mathematics courses once they entered college. But, as is the case in a pendulum system, the pendulum had already begun to swing. It is possible that, left alone, things would have been pretty good. As it was, the public reacted to the report, and the public demanded change. A *Nation at Risk* proved to be more influential than NCTM's report. However, it did not so much influence the period in which it was published as it established an environment that would be conducive to what was to come.

THE MATH WARS

And what was to come was the beginning of the math wars. This period in mathematics education began in 1989 and continues today. The pendulum swung to point E. Some call this period the time of NCTM. Others say that 1989 to 2000 was the time of NCTM, and that we should call from 2000 through the present the time of the math wars. Some argue that from 1989 to 2000 was the time of the math wars and we are now in the time of NCTM. Since the math wars are ongoing and NCTM is currently winning, I will label the entire period from 1989 to the present the "time of NCTM."

Whether you like my label or not, this current period began with the 1989 publication of NCTM's first set of standards. At that time constructivism became influential as well. (Constructivism is going to be explained in chapter 3. Suffice it to say at this point that constructivism is the idea that children must construct their own knowledge [and cannot learn when the teacher tries to transmit knowledge].) The NCTM became in 1989, and continues to this day, to be the most powerful influence on K–12 mathematics education in the United States. An entire chapter of this book is devoted to details of NCTM's standards. Another chapter is devoted to mathematics curricula inspired by the standards. Still another chapter is devoted to problem-solving in NCTM-oriented curricula. The following brief explanation will give just an overview of the situation called the math wars.

The 1989 standards (published by NCTM) call for a radically different approach to mathematics education. The NCTM was also influential in getting National Science Foundation (NSF) support. The NSF spent a ton of money on curriculum projects that supported NCTM. These curricula, called NCTM-oriented, are at the very heart of the math wars. (By the way, NSF continues to spend lots of money on projects that support NCTM.)

Let's return to the two sides of the math wars (one side being NCTM, supporting the NCTM-oriented curricula, and the other side disapproving of the NCTM-oriented curricula and wanting to return to the curricula in place before the math wars). The NCTM-oriented side calls for many things, including the following:

- Integrated mathematics curriculum (versus separate algebra and geometry, for example) with a little of everything in each year.
- Extensive use of calculators.
- Deemphasis on basic arithmetic.
- Increased emphasis on statistics and discrete mathematics.
- Continued emphasis (from the previous era) on problem-solving.
- Support for the concept that students must construct their own knowledge in order to learn. This leads to the promotion of self-paced learning, or discovery learning.

Let me say a little more about calculator use and the deemphasis of basic arithmetic. The NCTM-oriented side will argue that we should use a calculator for the same reasons that nobody would plow their fields using horses in place of a tractor. It is no longer important to learn how to plow a field using horses. But, the traditional-oriented side will give a different analogy. They will argue that, when one is out walking for exercise, one is unlikely to accept the offer of a ride. If one is walking for exercise, it makes no sense to accept the efficiency of a car ride. The efficiency and availability of cars is not the point when walking for exercise. Mathematicians will argue that whether a calculator is efficient and available is immaterial to whether a student should use a calculator. When students study mathematics, they are doing so for the mental exercise.

Note that mathematicians value other aspects of mathematics as well as the mental exercise aspect. The mental exercise aspect is a very important component, but there are many other components. The argument against calculator use also includes that mathematicians believe that by learning certain mathematical skills and procedures by hand, the student will better understand the foundation of higher mathematics. Thus, this goal of building a solid foundation goes beyond the mental exercise argument. Nevertheless, mathematicians very much value a student being able to master mathematics without depending on calculators. Calculators do have a place in mathematics education, and mathematicians certainly make use of calculators and computers. However, there remains a good portion of mathematics that mathematicians want students to do without calculators.

Turning to the deemphasis of basic arithmetic, the NCTM will disagree that they call for a deemphasis on basic arithmetic. But, they do! The NCTM wants to have their cake and eat it, too. The NCTM-oriented curricula (and the standards that were their inspiration) do not value any particular mathematics content. Rather, they want students to learn how to think mathematically. Mathematics includes algorithmic procedures. These are step-by-step processes that one can follow to solve a mathematics problem. These are often taught in such a manner that students do not develop understanding (the teacher just tells the students to do this, then this, then this, without explanation of why it works). Without understanding, the student will have to memorize the procedure. Memorizing a procedure is hard. So, a lot of students are not successful at memorizing procedures.

The NCTM could have called for teaching procedures with understanding, but they did not. Rather, they called for a significant decrease in teaching procedures altogether.

The NCTM claims that it is not true that they have called for a significant decrease in teaching procedures altogether. They agree that they do call for thinking about mathematics and that they want mathematical reasoning, problem-solving, communicating, representing, conjecturing, explaining, and many other -ings! However, they also claim that they STILL want the basics. My dad is fond of saying "you may want." That means that I want something that I am not going to get.

Time is finite. We like to tell each other, "I will make time for you." But, as human beings, we do not create time. We choose to let some things go in order to have time for other things. And that is what NCTM is actually doing. It isn't fair of them to say that they are emphasizing both. They are not.

The traditional side says that they approve of the things that NCTM is doing, but, there is only so much time in the day. Therefore, they choose to teach mathematics the way it was originally taught. Actually, more accurately, they would like to see mathematics taught the way it was, but even better. For example, do not teach procedures as memorization. Supporters of NCTM scream, why on earth would you pick a dreadfully dull approach, mindlessly shoving and heaving yourself forward through archaic procedures? Well, because learning to follow an algorithm is a life skill. It is important. And through the process, the content of mathematics will be taught and learned. Granted, the teachers need to attend to the "whys" of the procedures more than they have done in the past. Still, some things require practice, and practice takes time.

Note that those on the traditional side also often try to have their cake and eat it, too! The traditional side says that they teach concepts (understandings) as well as procedures. However, in the past, the traditional side has come up quite short on teaching with understanding. When the traditional side calls for a return to tradition, they actually want a return with some exceptions. Just as with NCTM, there is only so much time in a curriculum. The traditional side has not proven it can do it all, either.

So, neither side will have time for everything in mathematics. As a parent, you need to accept that. But, then you need to decide what is more important to you and your children. By the end of the book, you will know more and that will help you in making your decision.

The preceding discussion is not meant to say that NCTM is incorrect or that the traditional side is incorrect. There are fundamental disagreements between the two sides on what mathematics education is. In the course of the chapters to come, I will elaborate on both sides of the math wars. I think you will find that neither side is right or wrong, as such. Rather, each side values a very different part of mathematics. You need to decide what you want for your child, and that is the side for which you must fight.

In sum, it is important to see that mathematics education has always swung in this great pendulum swing. At one end is traditional, and the other is NCTM-oriented. Yes, NCTM-oriented is brand-new. But, is it? Certainly, the term is new. However, the thoughts were very present throughout history. Let us look one more time at our little line graph, and a repeat of the history: B, A, D, E, A, B, D, E. Although the idea of a time graph is my own, I have relied heavily on books and articles about the history of mathematics education in writing this chapter. The interested reader could do considerably more reading in this area.[9]

Table 2.1
A Timetable of Mathematics Education

Years	Name of Period	Characteristics	Place
Before the 1800s	The First Schools	Arithmetic	B
1800s	Mathematics for Mathematics' Sake	Math is very formal.	A
1880–1920	Practical Needs of Society	Math only as needed in direct practical applications.	D
1920–1950	Progressive Education	Nature of the child. Discovery learning.	E
1950–1971	New Math	Symbolism Formalism	A
1971–1975	Fads		
1975–1979	Back to the Basics	Basic Mathematics. Rote Learning. Drill, drill, drill. Cookbook mathematics.	B
1979–1989	Problem-Solving	No basic facts or drilling. Time is spent solving mathematics word problems.	D
1989–Present	The Time of NCTM	Math Wars. Constructivism. NCTM-oriented Curricula. Basics take a backseat. Extensive technology use.	E

A	B	C	D	E
	Traditional Side	Balance	NCTM Side	

SUMMARY

The history of mathematics education reveals a pendulum. Curricula and pedagogy has swung between two types: traditional and NCTM-oriented. At each point in history, it was believed that the current period was correct in its approach. At times, mathematics education was nearing success when the pendulum swung. At other times (such as during New Math), the curricula were such a disaster that it was important to have the pendulum swing. Table 2.1 provides a summary of the major periods.

CHAPTER 3

What Is Constructivism?

Constructivism, a theory of mathematics learning, is enthusiastically expounded by the NCTM-oriented side and unnecessarily feared by the traditional side of the math wars. The NCTM-oriented side of the math wars claims that before constructivism, mathematics educators did not understand how students learned mathematics and thus did not understand how best to teach mathematics. The traditional side of the math wars misinterprets constructivism to be a more radical theory than it actually is, and, in addition, assumes that constructivism is a practical theory (that is, that constructivism has influence on how mathematics is taught). Further, mathematicians on the traditional side of the math wars often feel that constructivism is incompatible with their beliefs about mathematics. The debates about constructivist theory have caused more misunderstanding than any other issue in the math wars. The purpose of this chapter is to explain what constructivism is as well as what constructivism is not.

Constructivism is one answer to the question: "How is it that students come to learn mathematics?" Which is a deeper question than "What are the actions that one takes to learn mathematics?" Students might answer the latter question with a flippant, "Study it." Actually, I consider "Study it" a much better answer than "Luck" or "One is just born able to do mathematics." Although "study it" might be an acceptable answer from students (it might even be a delightful answer coming from students), it does not explain what happens to enable one to learn.

It is true that there remain race, gender, and socioeconomic discrepancies in achievement scores on standardized tests in mathematics, which begs the questions: Is there a difference in how different people learn mathematics? Are some people inherently more capable of learning mathematics than others? There was a time when even our scientists believed that people learned mathematics only if they were born with a mathematical brain. Today some parents (perhaps unknowingly) express to their children that they may not have been born with a mathematical brain. This discouragement of children is unfortunate, as any K–12 grade child can learn mathematics.

Yet, we need to account for the discrepancies between, say, males and females. Actually, these discrepancies are easily accounted for, as these differences are very small, and sociological theories offer explanations. (See appendix 1 for a detailed discussion of gender differences in mathematics ability.) Parents, teachers, peers, and popular culture constantly send our children messages about the appropriateness of various people being good in mathematics. It is a serious problem in mathematics education that popular culture (movies, plays, literature, comic strips, television shows) presents mathematicians as either nerds or insane.

Let's take one area of popular culture as an example; consider all the movies you have watched throughout your life. How many had mathematicians as the lead character? If it is difficult for you to think of examples, it is because only a few movies have had mathematicians as lead characters. For purpose of discussion, we will consider three of them: *Good Will Hunting, The Mirror Has Two Faces,* and *A Beautiful Mind.*[1]

In *Good Will Hunting*, the main character is a mathematical genius but very disturbed psychologically. Yet, that character is not the mathematician I want you to consider. The mathematician I want you to think about is Lambeau, the mathematics professor who discovers Will. Lambeau is a self-serving social elitist. He is not a character that anyone would strive to be.

The Mirror Has Two Faces has a mathematician as one of the two main characters. He is portrayed as a sweet man but socially inept. His marriage proposal sounds like a mathematical proof, and the response at the end given by his intended is "Huh?"

In *A Beautiful Mind*, we are presented with a paranoid schizophrenic mathematician. Granted, it is a true story. The mental illness of the main character was not invented. Yet, it is unfortunate that the drama of mental illness is what it takes to find a mathematician interesting.[2]

If we send the message to children that it is unattractive to be a mathematician, we certainly do not encourage mathematics learning. Popular culture does play a role in mathematics learning. However, popular culture does not qualify as a theory of mathematics learning, because popular culture theory does not explain why some people learn mathematics despite societal pressure to not learn mathematics. While popular culture may explain the lack of popularity of becoming mathematicians, it does not explain how students are able to learn mathematics.

Several theories of mathematics learning exist that attempt to answer how all students (through all ranges of abilities and interest levels) learn mathematics. Note that the theories are theories of mathematics *learning*, and not theories of mathematics *teaching*. Yet, if we decide on a theory of learning, we ought to think about how teaching might be affected by the theory. If a theory does not offer teaching implications, then it is not a very practical theory. That being said, research has shown that often there is not a connection between pedagogy (how one teaches) and beliefs about how one ought to teach. Most teachers teach as they were taught (not as they believe they ought to teach or as they were taught to teach). Thus, even though constructivism is an issue in the math wars, and therefore it is important that you understand constructivism, it is debatable whether constructivism truly affects teaching.

Although constructivism is the only current mathematics learning theory being advocated, it will be easier to understand constructivism if you understand some alternatives first. The next two sections describe two alternative theories: cognitive science theories and sociological theories.[3]

COGNITIVE SCIENCE THEORIES

Under cognitive science theories, a student receives mathematical knowledge from a teacher (or another student) and reconstructs that knowledge for herself. The student may try to form connections between the new piece of knowledge and previous pieces of knowledge. The new piece of knowledge and all of the prior knowledge may become reorganized, or restructured, so that the new piece of knowledge becomes enriched, or possibly situated (that is, the knowledge is connected to the context from which it came). Some cognitive scientists believe that all knowledge is situated.

Let us consider an example in order to illustrate "situated." Researchers have found that the mathematics that students learn in classrooms is not the mathematics that students use in everyday life. Everyday life occurs in an environment—a cultural environment. Yet, the way that mathematics is taught in the schools is in a very different cultural environment. Some might say the cultural environment is a vacuum, but this is not possible. Regardless, researchers have found that the mathematics that one learns in school will not transfer to everyday mathematics (the mathematics that one does in one's day-to-day life). In many cases, students who are able to solve mathematical problems in the classroom are not able to solve the same mathematical problems on the job or even in the grocery store, and vice versa. It must be the case that school mathematics and everyday mathematics are treated as completely separate mathematics in students' minds. Apparently, students who can do mathematics in one setting and not another have not made the necessary connections between pieces of knowledge.

In the cognitive science theories, it is not assumed that students invent mathematical knowledge; rather, mathematical knowledge comes to them (possibly through a teacher). To learn, the student makes connections to prior knowledge. In this sense, the student is an active participant. It is not as if the brain is opened and knowledge is poured into the brain. *Learning* cannot be transmitted from the teacher to the student, and yet, teachers play vital roles both as givers of information and facilitators of situations that help students make the appropriate connections. If teachers believed in the cognitive science theories, they would purposely invent methods for easing the connecting process; for example, teachers might give students outlines of their lectures.

SOCIOLOGICAL THEORIES

Another set of theories can be grouped under a general label of sociological theories of mathematics learning. Sociological theories assume that students do not learn in isolation, but that they learn in the presence of other students and the teacher. It can even be argued that if a student is learning from a textbook, he is not learning in isolation, as he is figuratively in the company of the author of the textbook and all those who taught the author. Cognitive science theories also include some sociological principles (for example, the situated nature of knowledge), but they are not as dependent or enmeshed in the point of view as sociological theories are.

Sociological theories promote the idea that students learn mathematics by acting like little mathematicians and being enculturated into the field of mathematics. Students are apprentices. Students do construct their own knowledge, but they do so while interacting with others and being involved in mathematical activities. A "master" (the teacher) demonstrates a behavior that the apprentice (the student) models, receiving feedback and monitoring throughout the process. The master sets up situations and offers support for the students. Then, the master gradually withdraws support, and the students are able to do at least some parts on their own.

If teachers believe in sociological theories of mathematics learning, they might set up opportunities for students to interact with each other. Group work and other innovative teaching approaches would be used so that students would learn mathematics in a more participatory and interactive way.

CONSTRUCTIVISM

Let us move on to the theory that is in vogue today: constructivism. Constructivism is so popular that it is rumored that some mathematics education journals will not publish an article in which the author does not clearly subscribe to the constructivist theory. Roughly, constructivism is the idea that students construct their own knowledge. It does not work to have knowledge transmitted to students. It has become popular to say that the teacher must be a guide on the side, not a sage on the stage. Under constructivism learning theory, teaching as telling is ineffective, whereas teaching to promote discovery learning is effective. Constructivism promotes the idea that students must take actions, and then reflect on their actions. Through this process of action and reflection, students construct their own mathematics.

When constructivism is taken to extreme, it is called radical constructivism. Under the radical view, it no longer matters to teachers *what* students construct, only *that* students construct. For example, if a teacher believed in radical constructivism, she might suggest that a class discover a procedure for addition. Let us pretend that a class comes up with a procedure that does make some sense, but results in 2 plus 2 being 5. Under radical constructivism, this would be fine. The students constructed. It does not really matter what they constructed.

When constructivism is discussed in terms of mathematics education, it is usually not the radical version. It is usually not okay that a student arrives at the wrong answer. A more common version of constructivism for mathematics educators is social constructivism. Social constructivism believes that students construct their own knowledge in a social context. In other words, interactions between the teacher and students, and among the students, need to occur. Students still need to construct their own knowledge, and so problem-solving, and even creating their own strategies for problem-solving, is heavily encouraged. However, it is still important that students construct correctly.

In sum, constructivism states that it is not possible for a teacher to give knowledge to a student. Rather, a student must invent knowledge for himself. (Radical constructivism adds that it does not matter what they invent.) So, a teacher's job under constructivism is not as a giver of information. A teacher must facilitate situations so that constructions are likely. The other mathematics learning theories purport that a teacher can give information to a student, and then a student must act on it in order to learn it.

WHAT IS MATHEMATICS?

In order to understand constructivism more fully, and in order to understand why constructivism is not acceptable to one side of the math wars (the traditional side), the reader needs to understand a little bit about *theories of mathematics*. This is different from theories of mathematics learning. However, how one defines mathematics will affect which mathematics learning theory one accepts as truth.[4]

One theory is that mathematics is mathematics (that is, it just is). It is a product that one can set on the shelf and pick up as one desires. Mathematics under this theory might have dropped down from the sky. It is unchangeable. There is a correct, one and only, mathematics. It is the only mathematics that ever could be or will be. This theory is called Platonism.

Note that when Platonists view mathematics as unchangeable, this does not contradict the fact that new mathematics is "created" (Platonists would say discovered) often by research mathematicians. The body of knowledge (current understanding) of mathematics is changeable, but mathematics is not changeable. In general, the discoveries are made at an advanced level and do not involve K–12 grade mathematics.

Platonism and constructivism are not compatible theories. Although it is somewhat unpopular to say that one is a Platonist, I believe that many mathematicians are Platonists and very few mathematics educators are Platonists. A funny thing happened to me once when I was giving a talk on the subject of this chapter. I remarked that mathematicians do not tend to admit that they are Platonists, but I think that many secretly are. A mathematician shouted out, "I am a Platonist, and I do not care who knows it!" Since this man was normally a quiet man, I found this particularly funny.

There are other theories of mathematics, but they are less important for our purpose, which is to point out the true problem with constructivism as far as mathematicians are concerned (constructivism is incompatible with how a number of mathematicians view mathematics). But, we need to be able to see alternative theories of mathematics in order to understand better the Platonist view.

FORMALISM

Formalists believe that mathematics is a collection of formal rules. One needs to learn the rules, and learn how to operate within the system. From the formalist point of view, mathematics is not a product at all.

Let me illustrate this concept with something other than mathematics: consider chess. Is chess a product? There are the chessboard and chess pieces. Is that chess? Can chess be picked up and set on a shelf? The tools of it can. I can pick up the chessboard and pieces and set them on the shelf. Does it now make sense to say, "I have chess sitting on my shelf"? Or is chess a game that consists of rules and therefore cannot be picked up at all?

Having truth in chess might mean to follow the rules. If I do not follow the rules, it might be reasonable for someone to say, "But that isn't chess." I might still be using the chessboard and pieces, but "chessness" does not lie in the board and pieces. Further, there does not exist "chess" that could have dropped down from the sky. Many different versions of chess could have existed. If some other version of chess was invented and called "chess," we would not as a society rise up and say, "That isn't what chess was meant to be."

Parts of mathematics, under the formalist point of view, can be picked up and set on the shelf, but those are only the tools. Truly, what is mathematics, from the formalist's view, cannot be considered a product; rather, it is a very formal game, although the game may be meaningless. Does chess have meaning? Why do people play chess? To become chess masters? To enjoy themselves? The reasons to study mathematics are similar to the reasons for playing chess. Someone might study mathematics to become a mathematics master or just to enjoy the intellectual challenge involved in doing mathematics. Mathematics is made up of rules that one learns and masters. One can play mathematics. Yet, it is not a product. What defines mathematics under the formalist view is a process, and not an object to be set on the shelf. Further, there is no more mathematical truth than there is chess truth, unless by truth one means following the mathematical rules.

LOGICISM

Another view considers mathematics a logical system, consisting of logical rules. Truth in mathematics is guaranteed as long as one follows the rules. Everything in mathematics is broken down into logical concepts. Again, there is no mathematics to be set on the shelf. Logicism is very similar to formalism, except rather than mathematics being a game (as in formalism), mathematics is viewed as a logical system with logic and logical processes.

WHAT REALLY MATTERS TO MATHEMATICIANS?

There are many other theories of mathematics, besides Platonism, formalism, and logicism. Platonism is a very popular theory among mathematicians, but, despite what mathematicians say they believe, or even what they actually believe, there seem to be views that all mathematicians share. Mathematicians view mathematics as a systematic discipline that contains essential content and develops students' ability to abstract and to be disciplined thinkers. These components are present in Platonism, and sometimes violated by constructivism. Let us return to constructivism and to more details on why constructivism and Platonism conflict.

BACK TO CONSTRUCTIVISM

Under constructivism, the student is not required to find the "true" mathematics. Constructivism does not argue that there is no true mathematics; only that the true mathematics is unknowable. (I suppose this is similar to the difference between an atheist and an agnostic.) Constructivism makes it important that a student enter into the mathematical process and begin to construct mathematical images in her own mind. What exactly those images are does not matter. Only radical constructivism will go so far as to say it does not eventually matter what answer a student gets when she does arithmetic. Under less rigid forms of constructivism, a "wrong" answer still does not carry the same weight as a wrong answer under other philosophies. A wrong answer represents that the student has constructed, which is always good. In less rigid forms of constructivism, the teacher provides opportunities, so that the student adjusts her construction until the "correct" answer is formed. There is no truth under constructivism, and right and wrong take on lesser meanings in constructivism than in other theories. In Platonism, there is absolute truth, right and wrong.

Constructivism is a theory of mathematical learning, and not a theory about mathematics or about mathematics teaching. Technically, someone can believe constructivism and teach however he wants. However, if a teacher believes in constructivism and then teaches by telling, the teacher must also believe that his teaching is ineffective. Constructivists believe that children construct, no matter how a teacher teaches. Yet, if a teacher teaches in a certain way, then students should have an easier time learning. Although constructivism is not a theory of teaching, it calls for a new way of teaching.

The NCTM-oriented curricula are constructivist based; that is, a teacher does not lecture, or stress rote learning, drill, or memorization, or place an emphasis on procedures. Rather, teachers create situations in which students work in groups, discover mathematics, use multiple representations (for example, using a graphing calculator to work with a function's equation, graph, and a table of values), and experiment with open-ended questions. Later the teacher might make sure that the "regular" rules are "discovered."

Many mathematicians believe that there is a subset of mathematics that is not conducive to constructivism, because it is not conducive to discovery; therefore, that subset should simply be told to students. Mathematicians thus believe that some knowledge can be transmitted and do not subscribe to constructivism. Further, many mathematicians are Platonists, who believe there is one mostly knowable, true mathematics. (The word mostly modifies knowable because there is advanced mathematics that even Platonists acknowledge is unknowable; that is, the sheer number of logical steps needed to fully know it is beyond human ability to carry out. However, in general, K–12 grade mathematics is knowable.) Constructivism, with regard to mathematics learning, and Platonism, with regard to mathematics, are not compatible.

The goal of this chapter is to explain constructivism. Those who favor constructivism are on the NCTM-oriented side of the math wars; those who do not are on the traditional side of the math wars. This issue, however, has been made larger than it needs to be. Some parents fear that constructivism means that if their child says 2 plus 2 is 5, their child will be told "good job constructing," but that radical version of constructivism is virtually absent from the K–12 schools. Although some teachers will stress process over product, almost every teacher will also somehow let the child know that the answer to $2 + 2$ is 4 and not 5. Further, constructivism is not a driving force because it has not proven to be a practical theory. Most mathematics educators, even those who believe strongly in constructivism, will agree that what a teacher believes usually does not drive what a teacher does. Believing in constructivism is a method to justify pedagogy, and not believing in constructivism is a method to disregard certain pedagogy and accept other pedagogy. Therefore, arguing about constructivism is, literally, arguing about theory. It is probably a better use of time and energy to argue over other things (such as curriculum or pedagogy).

SUMMARY

Constructivism is a theory of mathematics learning. Its main principle is that students must construct their own mathematics knowledge. Teachers are facilitators, and do not give knowledge to students, as knowledge cannot be transmitted. Most mathematics educators believe in constructivism. The NCTM-oriented curricula are written to honor constructivism, but constructivism is not a practical theory; that is, it does not drive curricula.

Platonism is a theory of mathematics. Its main point is that mathematics is a product, and there is one true, knowable mathematics. Most mathematicians believe in Platonism.

Constructivism and Platonism are incompatible theories.

CHAPTER 4

What Does Research Say about the Math Wars?

Mathematics educators usually hold positions in education departments, in postsecondary institutions, where their job responsibilities include teaching, research, and service. The percent of time a mathematics educator spends on each of the three big tasks (teaching, research, and service) depends on the nature of her postsecondary institution. Many mathematics educators spend 40 to 70 percent of their time on research, the majority of which has produced supporting evidence for the National Council of Teachers of Mathematics (NCTM). And yet, this body of research has not ended the math wars, because education research is not definitive. This chapter will explain in some depth why it is that mathematics education research cannot be the final math wars answer.

Mathematics educators and other researchers (such as sociologists and psychologists) conduct research on the teaching and learning of mathematics. They attempt to give answers to questions such as, are the NCTM-oriented curricula successful? Are there gender differences in mathematics achievement? How should future mathematics teachers be educated? What topics should be included in elementary school mathematics? What strategies do algebra students use when problem-solving? How does technology, such as graphing calculators, affect students' learning of mathematics?

The list of questions is endless. Researchers form questions, design experiments, and attempt to find answers. The results are published in journals that other researchers read. Research is usually not written in a style that practitioners (such as mathematics teachers) are able to read. Elementary teachers, mathematics teachers, mathematics specialists (mathematics specialists are employed by school districts to make decisions regarding mathematics education for the entire school district), and administrators are among the people who depend on this research. Although these people probably do not read the research directly, they have two indirect sources: They go to conferences where the research is presented in usable form, and they read material from the NCTM that summarizes the research results in easier form. In both cases, practitioners do not hear or read enough of the research to judge its quality. Rather, they are given the results, and left to believe that the research results should be taken seriously, under the assumption that the research was well conducted and that the publication process is a fair one.

Mathematicians generally do not conduct research in mathematics education; mathematicians conduct research in mathematics. In order to keep their positions, mathematicians must produce a certain amount of mathematics research. After teaching and service obligations, mathematics research will use their remaining time. If mathematicians used time for mathematics education research, it would probably detract from their ability to move forward in their positions (to move from associate professor to full professor, for example). Therefore, mathematicians usually choose not to pursue research in mathematics education. If mathematicians want to know something about mathematics education, they ask colleagues in mathematics education or pick up information at mathematics conferences (which usually have a session or two about mathematics education).

Parents and all other laypeople have an even more difficult time finding information about mathematics education than do mathematics teachers and mathematicians. Parents hear about the research through mathematics teachers, administrators, or mathematics specialists, who are generally not reading the research directly; in other words, parents are two steps removed, not just one. Parents might hear about mathematics education at a Parent Teacher Association meeting, or they might visit websites that give information about curriculum projects and mention research for support.

All of this is problematic for many reasons. Unless you read the research directly, it will be distorted through the lens of the go-between.

Further, even reading the research directly is not ideal. Mathematics education research is anything but definitive. When one is studying human beings, the research design is not of a random, controlled study. When hearing or reading about mathematics education research, it is important to understand its limitations.

THE LIMITATIONS

The limitations of mathematics education research are so large that it is important to make decisions based on a considerable number of independent research projects. It is unwise to pick out any one research project and base decisions on the results. Because of the math wars, one of the most important research questions is whether the NCTM-oriented curricula are successful. These curriculum projects were based on research, and project personnel continue to do extensive research on student outcomes. The potential for bias in this scenario is enormous.[1]

It is a fact that the vast majority of research studies done about NCTM-oriented curricula are conducted by the very people who designed the curriculum. This statement is not meant to accuse project personnel of producing faulty or unethical research. However, it is a concern that researcher bias may occur to some extent when high-stake studies are being conducted by the very people with high stakes. This may not be (and most likely is not) a blatant or conscious decision, but researcher bias is a large problem in mathematics education research. Curriculum developers most likely would like to keep their jobs, to advance in their positions, and to gain reputations as quality curriculum developers. It is human nature to interpret research data in one's own best interest.

Researcher bias in studies of NCTM-oriented curricula versus traditional curricula can occur in several ways, and may not appear as a problem at first. It is common to have researchers pick teachers who most faithfully implement the NCTM-oriented curriculum. At first blush, this might seem appropriate. However, teachers are implementing NCTM-oriented curricula across the nation. If it takes a perfectly committed and extensively trained teacher to implement the curriculum successfully, then it should be considered whether the curriculum is a realistic curriculum to use. It would be better to attempt to select teachers in a random fashion so that the studies are not so much about what is possible as about what is actually happening. In deciding what curriculum should be used, it is more important to know what tends to happen than what is possible.

Even if the researchers are not biased, there is bias in the publication process. Mathematics educators who work as professors must publish research articles. To get a research article published, the researcher submits the article to one of a small number of mathematics education journals, where it is sent to three or four anonymous reviewers to ask if the article is a good one to publish.

Even though there is a shortage of mathematics educators, the research journals are overwhelmed with submissions. Journals publish anywhere from six to thirty articles a year. Every mathematics educator needs to publish at least an article a year. Journals are swamped with submitted articles. Most acceptance rates are around 5 to 10 percent of all received articles. This could mean that journals take only the very best articles. However, journals publish according to their own agendas.

In the same manner that I am not accusing curriculum developers of being unethical, I am not accusing mathematics education journals of being unethical. Mathematics education research cannot be definitive, for reasons that will be detailed later in this chapter. This lack of definitiveness causes every research article to be flawed in some manner— that is the nature of the beast. Further, it is human nature to find fewer faults with an article in which you like the results than with one in which you don't like the results. If you tend to think the results are true, it is easier to overlook the study's flaws. Imagine reading an article and thinking to yourself, "Gee, I hope that isn't true." Now imagine you find a flaw in the method. It is natural to say, "Whew, no, it isn't true. The study is flawed." This is the human condition. If you have grandchildren, are their faults as big as the neighbor's grandchildren's faults? I doubt it.

Recall that articles are selected because reviewers and the editor think that the article is worth publishing. The reviewers are people who have already published in the journal. The editor is well published in the journal. The most prestigious journal in mathematics education is published by the National Council of Teachers of Mathematics (NCTM). The others are NCTM sympathetic. Research articles that support NCTM have a much higher likelihood of being published than ones that do not. Of course, research that backs NCTM is not necessarily bad research; it may very well deserve to be published. However, research that does not back NCTM may also be very good research and deserve to be published. It is very difficult for that research to be published, however. It is important to be aware of both researcher and publication bias. Of course, researchers connected to these journals will scream, "Foul! If you write a really great article that does not support NCTM, I will publish it."

And that is where the conundrum lies. It is difficult to write a really great research article. There are pressures on the research process (besides the possible biases) that make mathematics education research difficult to carry out.

Let's use an example question to illustrate specific things that may go wrong. Let us say that we have a particular NCTM-oriented secondary mathematics curriculum in mind, and we want to know if students under that curriculum are better problem-solvers than students in a more traditional curriculum. Is it possible to delineate the skills we are trying to measure, design a test to measure them, administer it to students from both kinds of curricula, and analyze the results? Well, we can, but we will face some difficulties.

A large problem is that it is very difficult to control the variables. We want the only variable to be the curriculum: traditional or NCTM-oriented. But it is difficult to find a classroom that is just "traditional" or "NCTM-oriented," because teachers often supplement what they are doing with parts of another curriculum. And even if that does not happen, students may move between curricula or may be assigned to a particular curriculum based on their previous success in mathematics.

Then, we need to obtain sufficiently large samples. Each change in other variables narrows the size of the sample of students who can be tested while still maintaining a chance of obtaining meaningful results. Also working to diminish sample size are well-intentioned restrictions on research involving human subjects. I once sent out one hundred forms for parental permission to interview students for a study; only six came back with a signature.

Even if we could control the variables and obtain a large enough sample, it is very difficult to administer the measures consistently. I once arranged for secondary mathematics teachers in a variety of locations to administer a pencil-and-paper instrument to their students. Teachers' errors in following the detailed directions, and their false assumptions about the study, introduced inconsistencies that forced me to throw out the collected data.

Besides the researcher bias that I mentioned earlier, there is also a curriculum bias. There is no way of avoiding the positive effects created by the excitement and the special attention given to a new curriculum. Will these effects die out as the new curriculum becomes old? They may, but this is not measurable at the beginning.

These are just some of the obstacles to conducting research in mathematics education. It is impossible to create and carry out a perfect study. How many of the flaws get overlooked is up to the journals, and the journals support NCTM-oriented curricula.

QUALITATIVE VERSUS QUANTITATIVE

Another important issue concerning research in mathematics education is that there are two broad categories of mathematics education research: qualitative and quantitative. Unfortunately, this too creates a pendulum, in that there is no middle ground. A researcher could include some of both, and that is sometimes done, but generally a study is one or the other. Here is the rub: mathematics educators prefer qualitative, and mathematicians prefer quantitative.

Quantitative research occurs when numeric data are collected. Detailed statistical procedures exist so that the data can undergo mathematical analysis. Decisions are then made in an objective fashion. One is able to say that the data resulted in a statistically significant difference or not. Everyone in mathematics or statistics understands what this means—it is a very scientific approach. Mathematicians like the quantitative approach.

Qualitative research occurs when data are collected in terms of artifacts. Artifacts might be a transcript of an interview, open-ended questionnaires, notes from classroom observations, transcripts from discussion groups, or samples of students' writings about mathematics. These artifacts would not be scored, as there is no desire in qualitative research to have numeric data.

Qualitative research includes the case study. Each case study has only one subject, and so it is impossible to use statistical analysis (one needs a fairly large sample in order to apply statistical techniques). The researcher may attempt to give many descriptions, using rich language to paint a picture of how the student is thinking mathematically.

Qualitative research has detailed practices and methods, and is certainly not conducted haphazardly. If a researcher is going to conduct an interview, he does not just have a conversation with the person. Rather, he designs an interview protocol, which details what the interviewer will ask and what the interviewee is expected to do. The researcher will try to anticipate various responses, and the interview protocol may branch at various spots so that the interviewer will know what to do next no matter what the interviewee says or does.

Once the data are gathered, various methods of analyzing it are available. These methods are not statistical, nor mathematical. The researcher might give a narrative analysis of the data. The researcher might search through the data looking for themes, or categories, or data that repeat. Let me give you two examples of qualitative research.

I videotaped students from two curricula (NCTM-oriented and traditional) solving problems. Then, I attempted to find problem-solving themes. I concluded that the students from the NCTM-oriented curriculum were more engaged in the problems, more enthusiastic, had more ability to communicate mathematically, were more flexible in their solutions, and made less use of symbol manipulation in their solutions than the traditional students. (But I did not compare scores on tests. Actually by this method, I could find out things that I couldn't learn by just comparing scores on tests.)[2]

At another time, I was part of research team that collected a variety of data from teachers, trying to answer the question of how beginning mathematics teachers teach. We interviewed them, observed them teaching, and filled out classroom observation forms. Also, we had the teachers and students fill out surveys. Before the study began, we had created categories that interested us, and then when looking through all the collected pieces of data, we tried to fit the data into the categories, or determine that the data did not fit. One of the categories was what teachers do to develop as teachers. We then looked through the data and wrote such things as, "Many of the teachers stated that talking with other teachers was a factor that influenced their own development as a teacher." And, "By the examples teachers gave it was clear that their development affected their decision making about what goes on in the classroom." In qualitative research, one tries to pose and answer questions through descriptive data.[3]

Mathematicians are not comfortable with qualitative data, and they do not tend to take qualitative research very seriously. Qualitative research is used in the soft sciences, such as psychology and sociology, and not in the hard sciences such as chemistry, physics, and biology. This means that when one is arguing for the NCTM-oriented side of the math wars and using qualitative research to support one's points, some mathematicians will dig in their heels and argue that the research does not prove anything. On the other hand, mathematics educators much prefer qualitative research, and mathematics education publishers tend to publish qualitative over quantitative research. I once had an editor write that she liked my study, but suggested that, in order to get it published, I should redo it in a qualitative manner.

WHAT DOES THE RESEARCH SAY?

Mathematics education research is hard to do. It is difficult to get it published (unless it supports NCTM, and even then it is difficult to compete against all the other researchers). Mathematics education research has a lot of flaws, and it is not definitive. However, it is the best we have. We still need to look at the research when debating about issues in mathematics education. One should not simply accept the research blindly, but it is good to at least be aware of what the research conclusions are.

It would be impossible to summarize in this book all of mathematics education research. That would take many volumes. A book entitled the *Handbook of Research on Mathematics Teaching and Learning*, close to eight hundred large pages of small print, does attempt to summarize research in mathematics education.[4] The book suffers from the same problems that mathematics education research does. For one thing, the *Handbook of Research on Mathematics Teaching and Learning* is a project of the NCTM. But, for such a nearly impossible task, the book does well.

We are interested in issues around the math wars, and specifically how students perform in NCTM-oriented curricula as compared to students in traditional curricula. The previously mentioned book does not address that question. However, a new volume does. It is called *Standards-Based School Mathematics Curricula: What Are They? What Do Students Learn?*[5] This book is well done but has one huge flaw: The chapters in the book are written by the curriculum directors of the NCTM-oriented curricula.

It would have been much better to hire outside evaluators to write about the curricula.

The research shows that on most things, most of the time, NCTM-oriented students do as well as or better than students in traditional curricula. The NCTM-oriented students tend to do as well as or better than traditional students on "newer" content and processes. There is actual mathematical content (such as statistics and discrete mathematics) that is part of the NCTM-oriented curricula but is not included in traditional curricula. On that content, NCTM-oriented students tend to do as well as or better than traditional students. (Of course, that stands to reason.) On some processes (such as problem-solving or communicating in writing about mathematics), NCTM-oriented students tend to do as well as or better than traditional students. Again, NCTM-oriented students have more experience with these processes.

There is one area in which, some of the time, NCTM-oriented students do worse than traditional students. Almost never do NCTM-oriented students do better than traditional students in the area of basic skills. These basic skills include arithmetic skills (things that a calculator could do), but also algebra skills. NCTM-oriented students do not practice these skills as much as traditional students do, so this research result may also stand to reason.

Calculators can now do some of the algebraic procedures and manipulations that are taught in traditional Algebra I and II high school courses. Many students in NCTM-oriented curricula use calculators to perform these algebraic procedures and manipulations. These algebra skills are considered essential by mathematicians, including undergraduate mathematics professors. In addition, many mathematics professors will not allow the use of calculators in their classes. As far as mathematicians are concerned, it is a disaster if students cannot solve algebra problems by hand (without using calculators). On the other hand, mathematics educators tend not to value these same things, and rather, value the things of which NCTM-oriented students excel. The curriculum directors from one NCTM-oriented curriculum said this:

> On the whole, the evidence suggests that it is possible to streamline the traditional components of high school mathematics and incorporate important concepts and methods of statistics, probability, and discrete mathematics, while significantly improving students' understanding

of the mathematical content and its applications. A trade-off in somewhat lower traditional paper-and-pencil algebraic skills may result, although the revisions...appear to have reduced the deficit.[6]

In other words, there are lots of things that students in this particular NCTM-oriented curriculum do better than students in traditional curriculum. They might not do some traditional things as well (although the claim is made that revised material will help). And, this is an acceptable compromise to the directors. Herein lies the problem. It is not an acceptable compromise as far as most mathematicians are concerned.

It is difficult to decide on what side of the math wars the research lies. The research (although perhaps of questionable value itself) seems to come to this conclusion: the NCTM-oriented curricula are successful at what they value, and sometimes not successful at what they do not value. People who are NCTM-oriented will say "These are fine results." People on the side of traditional mathematics will think the results confirm our need to return to traditional curricula.

Supporters of traditional curricula will argue that studies have not yet been conducted to measure many important things. For example, we really do not yet know how students in NCTM-oriented curricula do in the long term (such as in college, in graduate school, and what percent of NCTM-oriented students seek careers in mathematics). In addition, mathematicians believe in the ability of the study of mathematics to make students into good, logical, clear thinkers. This mathematical thinking differs from the everyday thinking that is encouraged by NCTM-oriented curricula. Some supporters of traditional curricula argue that it is through the discipline of the by-hand symbol manipulation and procedures that students gain these thinking skills. Therefore, it remains to be tested whether or not NCTM-oriented students end up with solid mathematical thinking.

Obviously, it is important to conduct more research. A large study could be undertaken to examine two things: (1) Is it true that NCTM-oriented students have fewer of the skills that mathematicians want? (2) If it is true, does it make a long-term difference? (Are those students able to be successful in college? Are those students able to be successful in mathematics-intensive majors, and later careers?) It is also important that nonproject personnel conduct the research, and that the research attempt to be as close to "perfect" as possible. I will end this chapter with a suggested research project.

Give a large sum of money to a national set of researchers not connected to NCTM-oriented curricula—independent researchers made up of mathematics educators and mathematicians across the United States—to undertake a large study. A random selection of high schools should be taken. Mathematics classes should be examined by a subset of the researchers and rated on a traditional–NCTM-oriented continuum. Classes at each end of the continuum should be selected as being as representative as possible of the overall population. Participating schools that have both kinds of curricula would assign students to the curricula randomly. All participating schools would require that all students would be measured. A standardized test with a small quantity of open-ended problems and a corresponding rubric should be designed. The researchers themselves should administer the test in a consistent way. Multiple researchers should score each test, and a process of assigning a final score should be designed. These scores should undergo statistical analysis. This described study would not be definitive, but it is better than what has currently been done and would go a long way toward resolving the math wars.

SUMMARY

Mathematics education research is difficult to do. It suffers from many limitations. For example, it is nearly impossible to conduct a truly random experiment. Research studies that support NCTM-oriented curricula are easier to get published than research studies that do not. It is also a problem that researchers involved in curriculum projects tend to research their own curriculum. Most mathematics education research is qualitative. Most mathematicians prefer quantitative studies.

Existing mathematics education research studies support NCTM-oriented curricula and suggest that students in NCTM-oriented curricula do as well as or better than students in traditional curricula in almost every area that has been tested. The only exception is by-hand-symbol manipulation (of algebra equations) when these equations are presented without context.

CHAPTER 5

Who Are the Math Wars Players and on Which Side Are They?

The National Council of Teachers of Mathematics (NCTM) and their supporters comprise one side of the math wars. In 1989, 1991, and 1995, the NCTM created its first set of standards, made up of three separate volumes: standards on content and pedagogy, teaching, and assessment, respectively. In 2000 the three sets of standards were updated and condensed into one volume. The combined four volumes are very important, and an entire chapter of this book is devoted to detailing them. An additional chapter of this book is devoted to describing NCTM-oriented curricula. A third chapter describes the difference between NCTM-oriented mathematics problems and traditional mathematics problems.

In the four volumes of standards, the NCTM explains their vision, which includes mathematical understanding for all students. This means that all students regardless of race, gender, socioeconomic status, or future goals (college or not college-bound, interested or not in mathematics) should study some mathematics. The suggested mathematics is different from traditional mathematics curricula, and it needs to be taught in a different manner than traditional mathematics curricula have been taught.

The content of mathematics supported in the NCTM standards includes content that traditional mathematics curricula do not, such as statistics, probability, and discrete mathematics. In a nutshell, these topics deal with data analysis and topics that are important for computer science. They are not "traditional" topics in that sense.

The NCTM standards also recommend minimizing content that traditional mathematics curricula include. Minimized content includes symbol manipulation (solving equations for x, taught in algebra), formal proof techniques (such as two-column proofs, taught in geometry), and many (although not all) algorithmic procedures.

A result of the inclusion and minimization of certain content is that basic arithmetic skills and some by-hand symbol manipulation (solving algebraic equations with paper-and-pencil and not with the aid of a calculator) as well as many procedures in mathematics are deemphasized. The result of these skills being deemphasized is that increasing numbers of students are entering college without some traditional mathematics skills. However, these students are also entering college with some mathematics skills that students before NCTM standards did not have. One resulting issue is that college mathematics professors do not take advantage of the "new" skills, they assume that students have the "old" skills.

The NCTM standards also emphasize some processes that traditional curricula do not: problem-solving, communication, reasoning, representation, and connections. Problem-solving is solving nonroutine mathematics problems. Communication is talking and writing about mathematics. Reasoning involves mathematical arguments. Representation is understanding how to represent mathematics (with symbols, graphs, tables, and words). Connections are relationships among mathematical ideas, among mathematics and other sciences, and among school mathematics and the mathematics of everyday life.

The NCTM standards also promote use of technology (such as calculators) from the very earliest of grades, and in most (if not all) situations. The argument is roughly, if a calculator can do it, it should!

The new teaching methods promoted include group learning and projects. Open-ended problems with more than one answer and more than one solution process are preferred to the traditional problems, which have one solution path and the solution is a single numeric answer. The process of arriving at an answer is more important under NCTM standards than the answer itself. Students are to construct their own learning in order to remember and understand, according to the NCTM standards. The teacher as teller (and thus lecturing to students) is out, as it is not effective, says the NCTM standards. Rote learning, memorizing, and drilling are out. Teachers are facilitators of concepts. Students are responsible for building the concepts in their own minds.

THE TRADITIONAL SIDE

The other side of the math wars is supported by a hodgepodge of people, including many mathematicians. But, not all mathematicians are on the traditional side. Although a small number of mathematicians are on the side of NCTM, the largest number of mathematicians are on neither side (they are just not aware enough of the issues to pick a side). There are some parents on the traditional side. But again, certainly not all parents are on the traditional side. As you can tell, the traditional side is not organized with one organization, or even several, which fight for the traditional side. This is opposite of the NCTM side, which has, obviously, NCTM as its largest organization.

The best way to think of the traditional side is it is the opposite of NCTM. In one of the biggest differences, the NCTM promotes the use of calculators from kindergarten through twelfth grade. The traditional side promotes very little calculator use, and what use there is is found in the higher grades (certainly not in the elementary grades).

As for the content of traditional mathematics, it contains, well, *traditional* content: basic arithmetic, solving word problems (these usually follow an algorithm), other procedures, algebra, geometry, trigonometry, functions and function analysis (precalculus), and calculus (which students can take in high school or later in college).

Traditional mathematics curricula follow the pedagogy of going over homework, teachers presenting new material, and students practicing on exercises, which might include drill work. Students usually work as individuals. Problems have one solution process and one answer.

Supporters of traditional curricula think that the important content of mathematics is not covered in NCTM-oriented curricula. Further, traditional supporters think that students will not learn basic mathematics if students are in NCTM-oriented curricula, and, as a result students will not be prepared for college.

WHO ARE THE OTHER PLAYERS?

While the math wars consists of two clearly defined sides (NCTM-oriented and traditional), there are numerous people who have a stake in mathematics education and play a role in the debates at least from time to time. These players are not necessarily on one side or the other. For the remainder of this chapter, I will be describing these players and giving generalizations about their views. Of course, the key word in that last sentence is "generalizations." Any one individual is no more likely to hold any particular view than another person. The players may include:

- Students (K–12 and undergraduate students)
- Parents
- Secondary mathematics teachers
- Other secondary teachers
- Elementary teachers
- K–12 administrators
- K–12 guidance counselors
- K–12 curriculum directors and/or mathematics specialists
- School boards
- Parent Teacher Association groups
- Extracurricular groups (such as math clubs and math teams)
- Mathematicians
- Science and engineering college professors
- State-level versions of the National Council of Teachers of Mathematics (for example, in my state it is the Minnesota Council of Teachers of Mathematics)
- The United States Education Department, state education departments, the National Science Foundation
- Others in government, including politicians
- Standardized testing organizations (such as ACT and SAT)
- Mathematics educators
- Publishers
- People in the media (reporters for television and newspapers, for example)
- Businesspeople and other employers
- Grant writers
- Graduate students in mathematics education
- Other graduate students, especially those in mathematics

- Psychologists, sociologists, and others whose research includes mathematics education
- Everyone else who uses mathematics in their work or in their daily life (for example, doctors, nurses, pharmacists, carpenters, homemakers)

As you can infer from the last bullet, the list is everyone. Of course, this book cannot accommodate a paragraph description of the role that everyone plays in the math wars. In addition, any description of a group of people is by necessity a generalization. Most (but not all) mathematics educators are on the NCTM-oriented side, and most (but not all) of the mathematicians who have an interest in mathematics education are on the traditional side. (Many mathematicians are on neither side, because they are not aware of the issues.) One might wonder what motivates certain groups to take the position that they take. I believe that the main difference between most mathematics educators and most mathematicians is in the manner in which the two groups define mathematics.

For most mathematics educators, mathematics is a means to experience processes that mathematics educators value, such as thinking, problem-solving, communicating, conjecturing, reasoning, representing, and other higher-order processes. Mathematics is a means of experiencing, practicing, and perfecting these processes.

Although mathematicians certainly think those processes are wonderful, most mathematicians believe that those processes are not everything that there is to mathematics. Mathematicians view mathematics itself as a product as well as a means to processes. They value mathematics itself as an end (and not just as a means to an end). Most mathematicians will disagree strongly with curricula that contain only that mathematics that is necessary for the situations covered (that is, some curricula do not contain mathematics for mathematics' sake, but only mathematics that arises from real-life situations). Most mathematicians love mathematical procedures as much as they love mathematical processes, and they believe in simple, pure mathematical facts, including arithmetic facts. Most mathematicians like to learn as individuals and when they were students had no desire to join groups to talk about mathematics. They like to use problems that have one solution path, with one answer, while teaching, because then the students will learn the solution process. (Note that when mathematicians are doing research in mathematics, they do look for numerous solution paths to their questions of interest. The reader is not to infer that mathematicians prefer simple problems, but that they like to use these types of simple problems as teaching tools. In addition, mathematicians do join groups of other mathematicians and discuss mathematics.)

Mathematics educators and mathematicians also seem to differ on their view of K–12 education. Mathematics educators are interested in the mathematics learning of all students, including the not college-bound. Most mathematicians are concerned with the mathematics learning of the college-bound, and, in particular, of future mathematics majors and mathematics-intense majors. (More and more, mathematics professors are valuing the teaching of some "service" mathematics courses; service meaning mathematics courses for nonmathematics majors. Regardless, mathematics professors remain very concerned that future mathematicians are raised.)

Having these different views of mathematics and of the purpose of K–12 mathematics education is enough to result in different views of what mathematics curricula should be. If mathematics educators and mathematicians differ in these fundamental manners, then it really is not all that surprising that they are on opposite sides of the math wars. Although this may mean that neither side is right or wrong (each side is simply expressing different values), it does mean that resolution to the math wars will be difficult if left to these two groups. This is why it is so important to consider all the players.

Parents are the key players who need to be involved more in the math wars in order to resolve the math wars. Parents are students' best representatives. Parents have no personal agenda other than promoting whatever is best for students. In that sense, they are more impartial than mathematics educators and mathematics professors. At this point in time, those parents who are involved tend to be on the side of traditional. This is not to say that all parents have examined both sides and the majority have settled on traditional. Rather, those parents who are aware of the NCTM-oriented curricula either like it or not. If they like it, they probably do not become involved, because the NCTM-oriented side is in power, and it appears as if they will stay in power. Involvement does not appear to be needed if one is NCTM-oriented. Those parents who don't like the NCTM-oriented curricula and want to return to traditional will get involved on the traditional side. However, I believe that the math wars will get worse (nastier and more intense) before they get resolved. It is not at all a foregone conclusion that NCTM will win the math wars. Therefore, the future may see more involvement of parents on both sides, not just the traditional side.

Secondary mathematics teachers are the ones in the most difficult position out of everyone involved in the entire math wars. Other than students, secondary mathematics teachers are the most affected by the outcome of the math wars, as they have to do the teaching of the curricula. But, other than students, secondary mathematics teachers have the least ability to influence the math wars.

Schools are organized so that administrators, curriculum directors, and/or mathematics specialists make the decisions. Although mathematics teachers may be consulted or serve on committees, by and large, teachers use their time to teach. Administrators and the others mentioned use their time to figure out what teachers should be teaching. Decisions are made at the district level. Each individual mathematics teacher does not get to do what she thinks is best.

It is true that secondary mathematics teachers participate in local and state curriculum development, and in piloting materials, and in textbook adoption decisions, and certainly there exists teacher communication with building administrators, lawmakers, and parents. However, these roles are small compared to the forces of mathematics educators and the NCTM. Yet, if secondary mathematics teachers had a say, their say could eventually become a very powerful force in the math wars.

If secondary mathematics teachers could have a say, which side would they pick: traditional or NCTM-oriented? Researchers have tried to determine the answer to this question, and national surveys (with results that are published) tend to show they would pick NCTM-oriented. However, I believe that a large number (perhaps even a majority) of secondary mathematics teachers would actually pick traditional. I believe this for two reasons. First, recall that what is published is what supports the NCTM. Second, it is easy to answer survey questions in support of the NCTM-oriented side. For example, consider three possible Likert-scale items, with the scale being strongly disagree, disagree, neutral, agree, and strongly agree.

1. Secondary mathematics curricula should include many opportunities for problem-solving.

2. Students should be able to communicate about mathematics.
3. It shows an understanding of mathematics if a student can move among representations (tables, graphs, and equations).

Most secondary mathematics teachers would answer "strongly agree" to each of these items. That does not mean, however, that they would support NCTM-oriented curricula. It is similar to this: Respond to this statement with strongly disagree, disagree, neutral, agree, or strongly agree: "Poverty is not a good thing." Everyone would strongly agree. But, does everyone support the same government policies and proposals in order to prevent poverty? Most likely, no. Some of the statements made about NCTM-oriented curricula are similar to "Poverty is not a good thing," in that they are easy statements to support. But, it doesn't follow that everyone supports the playing out of the actual NCTM-oriented curricula.

Other secondary teachers are certainly players in the sense that they are affected by what happens. Science teachers are players, as they want their students to be able to do certain things. Although secondary science teachers like some aspects of NCTM-oriented (such as the problem-solving nature of it and the calculator use), they also want students who can do basic algebra. So, science teachers are a mixed bag, with as many science teachers on one side of the math wars as on the other.

Mathematics is not the favorite subject of most elementary teachers. They want curricula that are easy to teach. The NCTM-oriented curricula require more mathematics knowledge on the part of the teacher than traditional curricula do, because it is easier to tell students something than help them understand the *why* behind it. Traditional elementary curricula are full of basic facts and procedures. Elementary teachers know the basic facts and most of the procedures. They can tell students these things. But, if elementary teachers have to explain the *why* behind things, many of them cannot do so. The NCTM-oriented curricula are hard on elementary teachers, and most of them would like to return to traditional curricula.

The K–12 administrators, guidance counselors, curriculum directors, and mathematics specialists are mostly in favor of NCTM-oriented curricula. Most administrators do not have a lot of background in mathematics education or mathematics. They have a background in administration. Guidance counselors do not have a lot of background in mathematics education. They have a background in counseling. Curriculum directors do not often have a lot of background in mathematics education. Even mathematics specialists do not always have much of a mathematics education background. Because they lack background in mathematics education, they gather the research facts, assess the scene, and try to do for their school what appears to be the best thing to do. These people often (except the mathematics specialist) have to be experts in all areas. Of course, they cannot be that. They go to conferences, read journals, get on committees, and eventually believe what they are being told. Currently, they are being told by mathematics educators that NCTM is correct and that NCTM-oriented curricula are the way to go. So that is what they believe.

Another large group of people is affected by the math wars rather indirectly: college professors who are not mathematics professors, mathematicians who are not college professors, scientists who are not college professors, businesspeople and other employers, publishers connected to NCTM and not connected to NCTM, and media people. All of these players come in and out of the math wars. For example, a chemistry professor complains that students cannot problem-solve and finds himself supporting NCTM-oriented curricula. A chemistry professor complains that students cannot do algebra and finds himself supporting traditional curricula. Publishers have to decide what to publish and thus play a huge role in support of NCTM-oriented curricula, or in support of traditional curricula. The vast majority of what is published supports NCTM-oriented curricula.

Standardized testing tends to be traditional. There are several reasons for this, including that standardized testing is partially for the college-bound, and mathematicians (who are traditional) are sometimes consultants on standardized testing. This is not to imply, however, that mathematicians are generally supportive of standardized tests. Many mathematicians do not like the multiple-choice format of standardized tests, as they feel that students can work backward from the answers. Actually, mathematics educators do not like the multiple-choice format of tests, either, but for a different reason. Mathematics educators believe that the multiple-choice format does not allow for mathematical communication.

Another reason that standardized testing is traditional is that standardized testing was traditional before the NCTM-oriented curricula were developed, and it is difficult to change standardized tests. Standardized tests must go through validity and reliability studies, in order to answer the questions: Does the test measure what it claims to measure; and, Does the test measure in a consistent manner? Validity and reliability studies are expensive and complicated. One method for gaining reliability is to increase the number of questions. If the number of questions on a test is increased, the amount of time needed to take the test must increase, unless the questions are made rather quick to answer. Thus, a test is more reliable if the items require students to carry out a quick procedure. Quick procedures are more aligned with traditional curricula than with NCTM-oriented curricula.

Yet another reason that standardized testing is traditional is that standardized testing is promoted by politicians, and politicians tend to be traditional. But, perhaps the main reason that standardized testing is traditional is that standardized testing matched the traditional curricula in place, and how to now make them match NCTM-oriented curricula remains a puzzle.

I did a study once where I showed two tests to a group of mathematics educators. The tests were two versions of the same test, both originally multiple-choice. Both were respected national standardized tests. Measurement experts had made sure that the two tests were parallel (that is, the score a student gets on one will be the same score on the other, even though the items are different). From one of the tests, I removed the multiple-choice options, so that the test items had an open-ended format. I then asked the mathematics educators which test they liked better.

They all said that they did not like either of the tests, but they liked the open-ended test better than the multiple-choice test. They said that the open-ended test tested at a higher level, since students could not plug in the answer choices or guess at an answer. The experts also said that they thought the problems were less routine on the open-ended test than on the multiple-choice test. This could not be true, since the tests were parallel (I did not tell the experts that the tests were parallel) and the solution processes were identical from one test to another (even though the contexts changed). However, the experts thought that the solution processes were not the same, since on the multiple-choice test, students could work backward from the answers. In other words, these experts do not like multiple-choice tests.

As human beings, it is very difficult to see the good in what we don't like and the bad in what we do like. These experts saw the test they liked better (the open-ended one) and rated it higher on everything, even on attributes where it could not have been higher (for example, the routine nature of it, which had to be identical to the other test). Is this because the experts weren't very smart, or were unethical? Of course not. It is because they valued something, open-ended problems, and they placed their judgment with what they valued.[1]

In sum, the NCTM-oriented side is not fond of standardized testing because standardized testing aligns with traditional curricula. Further, to change standardized testing would be an enormous undertaking. For one thing, the format would have to change from multiple-choice to open-ended. Open-ended tests are expensive and inefficient, because of the way they need to be scored.

Actually, more than just the format of standardized tests would have to change in order to please the NCTM-oriented side of the math wars. The items will have to change as well. It will not be enough to simply remove the options from the multiple-choice tests, because test items conducive to a multiple-choice format are not the types of questions that NCTM-oriented people want. In the study that I conducted, the experts really did not like either test very much. I did not tell them that both tests were once multiple-choice tests. Even without that knowledge, the experts did not care for the nature of the items. Thus, it is not simply that experts dislike multiple-choice tests. Experts dislike the nature of multiple-choice questions, with or without the multiple-choice options. The items that NCTM-oriented people want cannot be answered with a single numeric answer, which is the case with multiple-choice tests, but also with many mathematics tests that are not multiple choice. The NCTM-oriented curricula have spent class time on class discussion, for example. Thus, they want test items that allow for discussion. This is nearly impossible in a standardized testing situation. The NCTM-oriented curricula have deemphasized any problems that result in one answer or whose answers could easily be obtained through a one-solution process, because these types of problems call for procedural solutions. Thus, the NCTM-oriented curricula have deemphasized any problems that are easily tested and have emphasized the very problems (thinking skills problems) that cannot easily be tested.

It is certainly reasonable of the NCTM-oriented side to want standardized testing to match their curricula. Of course, teachers should not teach toward a test. (Teaching toward a test means that a teacher covers only that mathematics that will be on a test.) No testing is able to cover everything, and reducing curricula only to information that will be tested is doing students a disservice.

Yet, testing ought to align with the curricula, or there is really no point to the testing. If the curricula is NCTM-oriented, standardized testing ought to be NCTM-oriented. At the current time, there is a disconnect, with standardized testing being traditional. Testing should not drive curricula, but curricula should drive testing. So, even the traditional side should admit that standardized testing needs to align with NCTM-oriented curricula during this period of time that NCTM-oriented curricula is in place. Until standardized testing aligns with NCTM-oriented curricula (or until curricula switches back to traditional), there will be numerous problems, with the disconnect between standardized testing and curricula a truly unethical situation.

Moving on to other players, the National Science Foundation (NSF) supports NCTM-oriented curricula. In fact, the NSF has funded the development of most of the NCTM-oriented curricula. The United States Education Department and most of the state education departments want to support NCTM-oriented curricula. State education departments set curricula standards, which support NCTM-oriented curricula. Politicians tell the education organizations what to do, and politicians tend to be traditional. (It seems tougher. *Tough on crime. High education standards.*) Standardized testing is done to meet the requirements of legislation. This creates another large disconnect between the required NCTM-oriented curricula (to satisfy state standards) and the required traditional testing (to satisfy legislation). School districts are supposed to produce students who do well on standardized tests, but have attended classes with NCTM-oriented curricula.

So, state education departments claim to be NCTM-based. But are they? We could go state by state and examine whether it is true that state education departments are NCTM-based. Let's do that for three states: Minnesota (my state), California (very important in the math wars), and New York (very important in the nation for setting mathematics curricula).

In Minnesota, a set of standards was in place called the K–12 Minnesota Mathematics Framework, which was very aligned with the NCTM-oriented curricula. In fact, it could not have been more aligned with NCTM standards. But, with a change in governors came a throwing out of the framework and a mandated revision to all statewide frameworks. The new frameworks are not in place as I write this chapter. However, the draft copies show a much less aligned curriculum to NCTM standards. There are no mandated textbooks in Minnesota, however. So, districts need to meet the state standards, but they can do what they want around that.

California is a very interesting case. An entire book has been written about the math wars just in California.[2] In the book, the author explains that in 1985 (four years before the 1989 publication of NCTM's first set of standards), the California Department of Education wrote a framework for mathematics teaching and learning in the K–12 schools. This framework could have been an earlier draft of NCTM's 1989 standards. Frameworks are supposed to last seven years, in California, and so a new framework was written in 1992. The new framework was very aligned with NCTM standards (which had just been published in 1989). In addition to the framework, California has a list of acceptable (adoptable) textbooks. Publishers realize that their textbooks must align very closely with the framework, or their textbooks will not be placed on this adoption list. Since California is very large, publishers want their textbooks on the adoption list. The textbooks that were written in order to align with the 1992 framework launched California into the math wars.

In 1995 the state superintendent of California formed a task force to examine the 1992 framework. The task force generated a report. Some say that the report called for a return to traditional curricula. Others say that the document called for a balancing of reform curricula with traditional curricula. Regardless of which of these is true, it certainly called for something much less NCTM-oriented than what was in place. Also in 1995, the legislature in California was well into the math wars, and they called for a back to basics approach and a moving back toward traditional curricula. (The nature of the math wars has been particularly brutal in California, with people on both sides actually receiving the threat of death unless they change their position.)

Long before the 1992 framework was through its seven-year cycle, there were calls for a new framework. The published 1999 framework is a very different framework than the two previous ones. Then again in 2000, a revised version of the framework was put in place (the current framework as of the writing of this book). The California Education Department says this about the 2000 edition: "This edition emphasizes the critical interrelationships among computational and procedural proficiency, problem-solving ability, and conceptual understanding of all aspects of mathematics."[3] So, the California Education Department is trying to say that the framework calls for a balance between NCTM-oriented and traditional curricula. But, the framework is not nearly so NCTM-based as earlier drafts of the frameworks, and it may even be more traditional than it is NCTM-based.

As mentioned, California maintains a list of acceptable mathematics textbooks. These are the only textbooks that can be used in grades kindergarten through eighth grade, unless a school prefers to forgo state funding. Districts can choose textbooks as they wish for grades ninth through twelfth. The textbooks on the adoption list are traditional in nature. None of the NSF-funded NCTM-oriented textbooks are on the list. Even when local districts in California get to pick the textbooks, they are to follow guidelines. If these guidelines are followed, traditional textbooks would be picked.

In New York, following a set of standards entitled the New York State Mathematics Core Curriculum is mandated. Seven key ideas that all curricula must include are given as well as guidelines on how to assess them. These ideas are named: mathematical reasoning, number and numeration, operations, modeling and multiple representations, measurement, uncertainty, and patterns/functions. The rule is this: "Each district can decide how they want to structure their program, as long as all the performance indicators and topics in the core curriculum are part of it."[4] A detailed document giving the core curriculum is available to anyone who wants it. The document is very much aligned with NCTM standards.

It is not worth the space in the book to go through all fifty states, for two reasons. As with Minnesota, as politics change, so will the state education standards. Information written in this book could rapidly become outdated. Second, the state departments do not control curricula as much as textbooks do. Some curricula will better match the state standards than others. If standardized testing matches the standards, and not the curricula, then there is a mismatch and students and teachers will struggle. But, this doesn't mean that the state is matching the standards. Overall, teachers will cover the textbook, and thus the textbook sets the curricula. Large states are thus important because of their ability to nearly control the textbook publishing industry. If large states all want a certain textbook, that is the textbook that will be produced. No matter what amount of arguing over the math wars occurs, eventually what matters is teachers close their doors and teach. But, what do they teach? Teachers are too swamped with duties to do much different than what is in the textbook.

The bottom line is, if you want to know what is happening for your child, find out what textbook is being used. Textbook selections normally go district by district (or sometimes school by school). Some states recognize that textbooks set the curricula. So, they mandate textbooks. They have a state adoption list of textbooks. This is what California does. Your child's teacher will know if your state has a mandated list.

In fact, asking your child's teacher questions is probably the best method for finding out whether your child's mathematics curriculum is NCTM-oriented or traditional. Simply asking whether the curriculum is NCTM-oriented or traditional, though, will probably result in the answer of NCTM-oriented. This does not mean that the curriculum is NCTM-oriented. Many curricula claim to be NCTM-oriented, but this is just a claim.

What has meaning is what is actually happening in your child's classroom. I suggest that you ask your child's teacher the official name of your child's mathematics textbook (the name that is actually on the textbook). Schools use various names for the courses. For example, the Core Plus Mathematics Project is often called Core Math or Integrated Math. Schools also use the same terms (Core Math and Integrated Math) to mean other curricula, and not the Core Plus Mathematics Project at all. Once you have the official name, go to the Internet and enter the name under a Google (or another search engine) search. Curriculum projects have websites. It will be fairly easy to tell from the website whether the curriculum is NCTM-oriented or traditional. Look a little deeper than whether the curriculum says it is NCTM-oriented. Almost every curricula will say it is NCTM-oriented. But, if you examine the website for what mathematics is included and what the students will be doing, it shouldn't be too difficult to tell if there is a true basis for the NCTM-oriented claim.

The bottom line of figuring out the players is to realize that although there are two sides to the math wars, there are also numerous players that have influence on what is actually happening. However, the textbook still has the greatest influence. To cut to the chase about whether your child's mathematics curriculum is NCTM-oriented or not, it would be most efficient to find out about your child's mathematics textbook.

SUMMARY

There are numerous players in the math wars. Standardized testing tends to be traditional. State education departments prefer NCTM-oriented. Politicians tend toward traditional. These forces create disconnects for students between what is taught and what is tested.

CHAPTER 6

What Are the NCTM Standards?

The National Council of Teachers of Mathematics (NCTM) is the most powerful and largest (over one hundred thousand members) professional organization affecting K–12 mathematics education in the United States. The NCTM, a nonprofit, nonpartisan mathematics education association, was founded in 1920, but came into a position of influence during the 1980s. They publish four professional journals. *Teaching Children Mathematics*, *Mathematics Teaching in the Middle School*, and the *Mathematics Teacher* are aimed at elementary, middle, and high school levels, respectively. The *Journal for Research in Mathematics Education* publishes, as the title implies, research on mathematics education. In 1989, NCTM released *Curriculum and Evaluation Standards for School Mathematics*. They also published two companion books, *Professional Standards for Teaching Mathematics* (1991) and *Assessment Standards for School Mathematics* (1995). In 2000, they published *Principles and Standards for School Mathematics*, which both updated and combined the three previous volumes.[1]

When curricula developers say that curricula is NCTM-oriented, they mean that it follows one of the two main standards volumes, the 1989 volume or the 2000 volume. Most NCTM-oriented curricula follow the 1989 version, because they were developed in the 1990s. Whether revised versions of curricula follow the 2000 set of standards is not always clear. Curricula developed in the 2000s most likely follow the 2000 version. The two versions (1989 and 2000) do differ in some important ways.

The NCTM (and their members and followers) comprises one side of the math wars. Although NCTM as an organization does not develop curriculum, its members do. Some of the members of NCTM have been supported through grants by the National Science Foundation (NSF) to write curriculum that is oriented toward NCTM. The writers of the curriculum are in agreement with the NCTM standards volumes and write curriculum that is in alignment with NCTM. The NSF is also in agreement with the NCTM standards volumes, and that is why they offer grant money for projects that promote NCTM views and standards.

WHY HAVE STANDARDS?

The NCTM presents a three-pronged case to support the need for the mathematics standards. First, the world is changing rapidly. The world was very different in 1989 from what it was fifteen years before that. Today's world is very different from what it was in 1989. Technology is changing. Calculators are becoming cheaper, smaller, and more powerful. Graphing calculators can, obviously, graph. Some calculators have what is referred to as "CAS" capabilities. The CAS stands for computer algebra systems, and this literally means that the calculator can do algebra. The NCTM believes that technology is changing what skills students need to have. Further, the skills that employers require from employees have changed. Employers want employees who can problem-solve more than they want employees who can do procedures in mathematics. In the workplace, the procedures in mathematics have largely been replaced with technology. Because the world is changing, the mathematics that all students need (and not just the college-bound) is also changing.

Second, students today are different. Students like technology, and grow up using technology, including the World Wide Web. Students are used to the sophistication and pace of technology. Today's students have and want quick access to visual information.

Third, mathematics education has not been successful. Our students do not compete well with students from other nations. Our students cannot problem-solve. Within the United States, there are large discrepancies from state to state in students' mathematics abilities.

The four volumes—*Curriculum and Evaluation Standards for School Mathematics* (1989), *Professional Standards for Teaching Mathematics* (1991), *Assessment Standards for School Mathematics* (1995), and *Principles and*

Standards for School Mathematics (2000a)—are NCTM's response to the three issues discussed in the preceding paragraph. Previous NCTM documents (such as *An Agenda for Action* mentioned in chapter 2) set the groundwork for the publication of the four standards documents. The standards have been enormously popular with mathematics educators. Almost without exception, any current curriculum with a hope of being adopted by a school needs to at least claim to be NCTM-oriented. And the very few curricula that call themselves traditional demonstrate how they meet NCTM standards. Of course, there still exist those people on the other side of the math wars who argue against the NCTM-oriented curricula, but currently they have little power in K–12 schools.

The rest of this chapter will describe the four sets of standards. Even though the 2000a document is an update of the others, it is important to describe all four documents. The spirit of the 1989 document, in particular, differs from the spirit of the 2000a document. The details also differ.

THE 1989 STANDARDS

The 1989 standards make it clear that the teaching of mathematics needs to change. It directly states that: "All students need to learn more, and often different, mathematics and that instruction in mathematics must be significantly revised."[2] The 1989 standards are intended as a vehicle for change and not an endorsement, by any means, of the status quo. Put in simple language, the standards aim to promote a new philosophy of mathematics education and gain room for the new by decreasing attention to the old. Basic skills, computation, procedures, and symbol manipulation (algebra) are all included in the old that need to get out of the way in order to make room for the new.

The new issue that the 1989 standards want to promote is mathematics as a process and not a product. No particular content in mathematics matters all that much in the 1989 standards. Rather, it matters that students begin to involve themselves with mathematical processes. Rather than teaching students procedures for solving problems, teachers should pose questions to the students. These open-ended questions contain opportunities for mathematical problem-solving. It is then up to the students to enmesh themselves in thinking about the problem. Over time, it is hoped and predicted that students will learn how to model mathematically (how to use mathematics to consider and solve real-life problems). Mathematics becomes a process that students can use in life.

Included in this philosophy is the idea that only those who eventually become mathematicians need the traditional algebraic skills. Therefore, the reasoning is that traditional curricula are not appropriate for the majority of students. The 1989 standards state that those students who do continue in mathematics can easily pick up what they lack once they enter college. If nothing else, they can probably teach to themselves whatever it is that they lack.

These claims that students can later pick up the missing traditional skills (and even at a quicker pace than students would have learned them at the beginning) are backed by mathematics education research. However, mathematicians are skeptical about this research and believe that students will not learn the traditional algebraic skills if they are not emphasized in high school. Further, mathematicians are not willing to teach these skills at college, or at least not in the regular series of mathematics courses. When a student enters calculus in college, for example, mathematicians do not want to be teaching algebra to them. Therefore, the students truly are left to learn the missing skills themselves. Mathematics education research does not back up the idea that students can teach *themselves* algebra later and have it all come out okay. Actually, this part of the 1989 standards was debated enough that the reader will notice changes in it when we discuss the 2000 version of the standards.

The 1989 standards are organized into three gradebands: kindergarten through fourth, fifth through eighth, and ninth through twelfth. The standards differ for each of the three gradebands. The goals, positions, and philosophies, however, do not differ across gradebands. The 1989 standards state that students learn through being actively involved and that constructivism needs to be reflected in the pedagogy. (We discuss constructivism in chapter 3 of this book.) Group work, discussions, and project work are all necessary pedagogical techniques in the mathematics classroom, according to the 1989 standards. Computations should not be the focus of mathematics, and the traditional sequence of courses (algebra, geometry, precalculus, and calculus) is not appropriate for most students.

All three gradebands have the first four standards in common: mathematics as problem-solving, mathematics as reasoning, mathematics as communication, and mathematical connections. These four standards are labeled the process standards and are at the heart of how the 1989 standards define mathematics.

Problem-solving is defined as the solution process entered when the path is not obvious. Therefore, solving a routine problem using a taught procedure is not problem-solving. The 1989 standards call for an increased emphasis on problem-solving and, in fact, problem-solving becomes the main activity of students. It is important to understand that this constitutes a major change in mathematics curricula. Traditional mathematics curricula include problem-solving, but also include arithmetic, computational processes, and a good deal of procedural algorithms. Problem-solving and procedures are two different things. Learning to problem-solve is like filling a bag with mathematical strategies, not with mathematical procedures. A good problem-solving strategy is to guess and then check one's guess. Another strategy is to start at a possible solution and work backward through the problem to see if it is a solution. Another strategy is to try simpler cases, and then see if a pattern develops. There are literally hundreds of problem-solving strategies, but these strategies differ from learning mathematical procedures (such as how to solve an equation).

Learning problem-solving techniques is good, but there is only so much time in the school year. If problem-solving replaces other content, the loss of that content has consequences. Algebra is a discipline of mathematics that is valued by mathematicians. However, algebra is not considered problem-solving by the 1989 standards, and thus is considered much less important. In fact, the two most important topics in K–12 mathematics according to mathematicians are arithmetic and algebra skills. Both of these areas are to be deemphasized and replaced with other skills, such as problem-solving, according to the 1989 standards. While all curricula include problem-solving, NCTM-oriented curricula make room for problem-solving at the expense of other content. Because problem-solving is a large component of NCTM-oriented curricula, an entire chapter of this book is devoted to explaining the different characteristics of problem-solving under NCTM-oriented curricula and under traditional curricula.

Mathematics as communication is the requirement that students express their mathematical thinking through language (both verbal and written). Students should explain their answers in words as well as describe their strategies for forming these answers. Students need time for reflection, explanations, and justifications of their answers. Students have to engage in mathematical thinking and show, through some method of communication, that they are thus engaged. It is this communication standard that makes standardized testing difficult, as standardized testing is commonly of multiple-choice format, which does not allow for communication of mathematics. Further, this communication standard is virtually absent in traditional mathematics curricula. The bottom line is that mathematicians do not value communication, as defined by NCTM, all that much. Mathematicians view problem-solving itself as mathematical communication and do not require that students write out their solution process in words. This transfer to English words is assumed by mathematicians, but is usually not required in writing.

Mathematics as reasoning calls for students to make mathematical conjectures and mathematical arguments. Also, students should develop their ability to reason and apply proof techniques. However, these proof techniques are not the same proof techniques that mathematicians use and value. Rather, the proof techniques are methods of verification that mathematicians do not accept as proof.

The connections standard calls for students to see the connections among mathematical ideas as well as throughout the entire K–12 mathematics curricula and among nonmathematical subjects. In addition, students should be able to apply school mathematics to everyday life.

The 1989 standards give separate content standards for each gradeband. In the K–4 gradeband there are nine content standards: estimation, number sense and numeration, concepts of whole number operations, whole number computations, geometry and spatial sense, measurement, statistics and probability, fractions and decimals, and patterns and relationships. Perhaps more informative than going through each of these content areas and listing details on what each contains is to identify what the 1989 standards say not to do. The 1989 standards call for "decreased attention"[3] to several topics within mathematics. Unfortunately, many curricula directors took "decreased" to mean "none."

In the early gradeband, less attention should be given to complex paper-and-pencil computations, isolated treatment of paper-and-pencil computations, addition and subtraction without renaming, isolated treatment of division facts, long division, long division without remainders, paper-and-pencil fraction computation, use of rounding to estimate, primary focus on naming geometry figures, memorization of equivalencies between units of measurement, and use of clue words to determine which operation to use. The 1989 standards also call for decreased use of rote practice, rote memorization or rules, problems that result in one answer or one method for finding the answer, use of worksheets, written practice, and teaching by telling.[4]

These are major shifts in teaching and content. Much of the 1989 standards call for a decreased emphasis on arithmetic skills and operations, which are the core of the traditional elementary curricula. For example, the 1989 standards state that long division can be accomplished through a calculator. However, many mathematicians believe that it is through long division that students learn the base number system. In the United States, we use the Hindu-Arabic number system. This number system has many amazing components. For example, we can represent any number we want by using only ten digits (0, 1, 2, 3, 4, 5, 6, 7, 8, and 9). We have the number 0, and it can be used to hold a place in our place-value system. For example, 501 is a different number than 51. Our number system is a base-10 system, so the number 12045 really means we have 5 units, 4 tens, 0 hundreds, 2 thousands, and 1 ten thousand, or as a sum: $5 + 4 \cdot 10 + 0 \cdot 10^2 + 2 \cdot 10^3 + 1 \cdot 10^4$ or $5 + 4 \cdot 10 + 0 \cdot 100 + 2 \cdot 1000 + 1 \cdot 10000$, where I have used dots to represent multiplication.

It is really important that students understand the place-value system. Procedures like long division or converting between bases (for example, using a base-3 system instead of a base-10 system) are opportunities for explaining the concepts of a place-value system. Mathematicians do not so much value long division as they value the opportunity for students to come to deeper understandings about mathematics.

However, if elementary teachers themselves do not know how to teach long division in such a manner that the base number system is taught, then they will teach long division as an algorithm. When it is taught as an algorithm, it is debatable whether the calculator replacing it matters that much. However, the 1989 standards do not call for "better" teaching of long division. Rather, the 1989 standards call for "decreased" teaching of long division.

The middle gradeband has some standards in common with the elementary gradeband, but even so the emphasis is different. The middle gradeband has nine content standards: number and number relationships, number system and number theory, computation and estimation, patterns

and functions, algebra, statistics, probability, geometry, and measurement. The 1989 standards emphasize that basic skills are not the point of
the middle gradeband. If students do not have the basic skills by middle
school, then they should use a calculator and get on with mathematics,
according to the 1989 standards. (Basic skills include the addition, subtraction, multiplication, and division of numbers.)

The decreased attention section is significant. It calls for decreased
attention to almost everything that was traditionally in the middle set of
grades. In particular, decreased attention is to be given to memorizing
rules and algorithms, practicing "tedious" paper-and-pencil computations, and finding exact forms of answers. All of these skills are at the
heart of what mathematicians value.[5] Of course, mathematicians would
likely object to the 1989 standards' use of the word "tedious," and it is
difficult to define just what makes a computation tedious or not. A
concrete example may add some clarity. The NCTM standards consider
computation with fractions a tedious operation, while mathematicians
think it is essential that students can compute with fractions. Here is a
quote from the 1989 standards:

> The mastery of a small number of basic facts with common fractions (e.g.,
> $1/4 + 1/4 = 1/2$; $3/4 + 1/2 = 1\ 1/4$; and $2\ 1/2 \times 1/2 = 1\ 1/4$) ... contributes
> to students' readiness to learn estimation and for concept development
> and problem solving.... This is not to suggest, however, that valuable
> instruction time should be devoted to exercises like $17/24 + 5/18$ or
> $5\ 3/4 \times 4\ 1/4$, which are much harder to visualize and unlikely to occur in
> real-life situations.[6]

Mathematicians are extremely opposed to the above. Mathematicians
believe that it is essential that students can compute things such as
$17/24 + 5/18$ or $5\ 3/4 \times 4\ 1/4$. Regardless of the possible disagreement
over the definition of tedious, the 1989 standards want fewer tedious
computations.

The algebra standard calls for decreased emphasis on manipulating
symbols. However, manipulating symbols is at the core of traditional algebra. The 1989 standards promote solving linear equations through other
methods, such as using a graphing calculator and then finding the in-
tercept. Memorizing takes on a bad name under the 1989 standards.
Mathematicians believe that memorizing a small set of mathematical

procedures enables one to later (perhaps at the undergraduate level) use those skills to build mathematics that is more powerful. It is true, though, that NCTM-oriented curricula attempt to serve all students, and not exclusively the college-bound. However, in doing so, the college-bound are often left not being appropriately served.

The last gradeband has ten content standards: algebra, functions, geometry from a synthetic perspective, geometry from an algebraic perspective, trigonometry, statistics, probability, discrete mathematics, conceptual underpinnings of calculus, and mathematical structure. Decreased emphasis on the traditional methods of teaching algebra, geometry, trigonometry, and functions are all stressed. For example, in geometry, much of the traditional course is spent on proofs. In NCTM-oriented, proofs are to be replaced with deductive arguments.

Overall, the 1989 standards promote additional mathematics content in K–12 grades, such as discrete mathematics, statistics, and probability. In addition, three of the process standards (problem-solving, reasoning, and connections) are not a large part of traditional mathematics curricula. And, communication, the fourth process standard, is absent from traditional curricula. Both the content and process additions are positive additions. However, K–12 mathematics curricula are already full. In order to fit more in, other things have to go.

The main area that the standards suggest in order to make room for the additions is in procedural and computational mathematics. Computational mathematics is what you would expect; that is, doing arithmetic computations. The NCTM labels computational mathematics as paper-and-pencil mathematics without a context. Mathematicians are not as concerned with having a context as NCTM is. Computational mathematics includes basic mathematics such as long division and multiplying decimals. Procedural mathematics is a step-by-step procedure, algorithm, or recipe for solving a problem. The NCTM tries to promote conceptual understanding instead of procedural understanding. Conceptual understanding includes understanding how to solve mathematics problems that are nonroutine to the student. If a student follows a planned course of action for solving certain problems, that is considered procedural. But, if the student follows directions and does not understand what he is doing, it is unlikely that the student could apply the procedure to a new version of the problem (one that differs a little). Conceptual versus procedural has created a false pendulum in the math wars. Some people think that procedural is on the side of traditional, and conceptual is on the side of NCTM-oriented. Actually, the traditional side wants both conceptual and procedural. The NCTM wants the majority of emphasis on conceptual, but some procedural as well. However, it is true that a main difference between the traditional side and the NCTM side lies in how much the procedural is valued. The traditional side values procedural much more.

This decreased emphasis on computations and procedural skills follows into the manner in which NCTM wants algebra and other mathematics to be taught. Algebra under the traditional viewpoint consists of working with symbols and manipulating symbols by hand to solve equations. This is mathematics without a context, and the 1989 standards want much less emphasis placed on this skill. Mathematics professors value algebraic skills. How much to value the ability to manipulate symbols not set in a real-life context is a major disagreement between the two sides in the math wars. Further, whether or not symbol manipulation ability matters plays itself out in placement into college mathematics courses. Placement tests are written by mathematics professors and are usually very algebraic in nature. Students from NCTM-oriented curricula will not do as well on these tests as students from traditional curricula. (See appendix 3 for more information about placement testing.)

Another stand taken by the 1989 standards is the call for technology use in all grades, even kindergarten. At times (such as in the middle gradebands) the standards suggest that the calculator should do the basic arithmetic that students cannot do in order for the students to move ahead with their mathematics learning. At other times, the calculator is meant to replace "tedious" arithmetic skills. Always, it is intended that calculators replace time-consuming computations. In addition, the calculator is intended to add depth to students' understanding. For example, a student examines an equation. Rather than just solve it with paper-and-pencil, the student could use a graphing calculator to both graph it and generate a table of values. By moving between these representations (equation, graph, and table), it is hoped and predicted that the student will have a richer and deeper understanding of the mathematics. Unfortunately, to gain the time to create these additional representations, time is taken from the paper-and-pencil practice.

Finally, the 1989 standards clearly call for new pedagogy in mathematics teaching. The teacher as teller is out, and the teacher as a guide is the replacement role. Discussion in mathematics is promoted (discussion is absent from traditional pedagogy). Group work is a suggested method for playing out the constructivist philosophy that the 1989 standards support.

STANDARDS FOR TEACHING

Soon after the 1989 standards, NCTM followed with *Professional Standards for Teaching Mathematics*. This document spells out in no uncertain terms that mathematical pedagogy needs to change. Mathematics classrooms are to work as classes and not have students working as individuals. The teacher is to step down as the authority, and students are to learn to construct their own mathematical knowledge, through logic, mathematical evidence, and reasoning. Memorizing procedures is not good use of class time. Students should conjecture, invent, problem-solve, and form connections between mathematical topics and other subjects. Spending class time on discussions is promoted as a very good use of time.

The document also describes methods for evaluating the teaching of mathematics and how professional development for mathematics teachers ought to occur. These issues, while important in their own right, are not as important for our understanding of the math wars.

STANDARDS FOR ASSESSMENT

The next document is the *Assessment Standards for School Mathematics*. This document puts forth six standards. The mathematics standard states that assessment ought to assess what we want students to know. At first blush, it may seem like an obvious statement that teachers should test what was taught. However, two points are important to make.

First, the assessment document is careful to use the word "assessment" versus the word "test," because standardized tests and college placement tests tend to emphasize the very things that the NCTM-oriented side wants deemphasized. Therefore, NCTM-oriented students do not do as well on these measures as traditional students. For that reason, the NCTM-oriented side would like tests to be less important.

Second, besides not wanting tests to count so much, the NCTM-oriented side would like other measures to count more. For example, the NCTM-oriented side argues that mathematical discussion is important, and that class time ought to be spent on it. Therefore, if we believe that what is taught ought to be tested (assessed) and what is tested ought to be taught, then there should be assessment of classroom discussion. Assessment of discussion is difficult to do, time-consuming, and expensive. Interviews might accomplish assessment of discussion, but then one needs a qualified interviewer (the teacher is most likely busy with the class) and the time to conduct the interviews. But, under this type of assessment, NCTM-oriented students usually do much better than traditional students. Thus, making a standard that says "assess what you teach" is more important than it first appears for promoting NCTM-oriented curricula.

The rest of the standards in this document are more straightforward. The second standard states that assessment itself should cause students to learn. This is a justification for the amount of time that will be needed for assessment. The third standard calls for equity for all under the assessment practices. The fourth states that assessment should not be kept a secret, but be an open process. The fifth standard states that valid inferences about learning should be made following assessment. Finally, the last standard calls for a coherent assessment system. Although one should not teach to the test, there should be a consistency between what is tested and what is taught. There should not be content on the test that was not taught, and for the most part, what was taught should be tested.

Other parts of the assessment document call for using assessment for a variety of purposes, not just for grading. The document calls for assessment for monitoring students' progress, making instructional decisions, evaluating students' achievement, and evaluating programs.

The main point of the assessment document is to move assessment away from the traditional forms of testing, so that NCTM-oriented students have a better chance of showing what they know. This, of course, is only logical. We really ought to be testing what we value. What happens in the math wars, though, is that in the testing of mathematics, we are able to see what we value. It is one thing to talk about changes in mathematics teaching and learning. But, if these changes mean that students will not do as well on standardized tests (including the ACT and the SAT) and on college placement tests, then either this testing or the NCTM-oriented curricula should change. Of course, the NCTM-oriented side would prefer that the testing change, while the traditional side defends what the tests are testing and prefer that NCTM-oriented curricula change.

THE 2000 DOCUMENT

This brings us to the 2000 set of standards. The *Principles and Standards for School Mathematics* is an updated version of the 1989 standards, and a combining of the other two documents. Many things are the same, but some important things differ. The entire document is simplified by having the same ten standards for all grades K–12.

The 2000 standards consist of five content standards and five process standards. The content standards are number and operations, algebra, geometry, measurement, and data analysis and probability. The process standards are the same four from the 1989 standards (problem-solving, reasoning and proof, communication, and connections) and one additional one, representation. The standards and principles are applied across four gradebands (in 1989 it was three gradebands): prekindergarten through second, third through fifth, sixth through eighth, and ninth through twelfth. The emphasis of the individual ten standards varies across the gradebands. For example, number and operation has a higher emphasis in the lower grades than in the upper grades, and algebra has a higher emphasis in the upper grades than in the lower grades. There are also six principles: equity, curriculum, learning, teaching, assessment, and technology.

The equity principle calls for all students to receive equal opportunities in mathematics. Although the equity principle does not call for the exact same curriculum for each student, it does call for fairness in opportunities to learn mathematics. The equity principle also states that every student should take mathematics every year from prekindergarten through twelfth grade.

The curriculum principle speaks against curriculum that is a variety of topics and situations, and for a curriculum that is consistent and well thought out from prekindergarten to twelfth grade. The curriculum principle calls for a purposeful connection between the separate courses in mathematics. In other words, mathematics is a subject that builds, and yet the courses are treated as if there are no explicit connections. Connections need to be made explicit to students. Mathematicians seem to believe that the connections are obvious to students, but the connections are not obvious at all. For example, most traditional students mistakenly believe that algebra and geometry have nothing to do with one another.

The teaching principle calls for qualified mathematics teachers, both in terms of mathematics content and of understanding pedagogy that promotes learning. The principle states that teachers must continue to learn about teaching even after they have graduated through continual professional development.

The learning principle is that students need to be active learners, not passive, and that learning must build on the knowledge that students currently have. There is also a call for a concentration on learning conceptually instead of procedurally.

The assessment principle calls for assessment that aligns with the curriculum. This has played out to be a deemphasis on testing, or at least testing in the traditional manner. The principle calls for assessment through other means, such as essays.

The technology principle calls for technology for every student. This is the same as in the 1989 standards.

The number and operations standard calls for basic computational fluency. This standard might be what you would call arithmetic.

The algebra standard calls for elementary students working with patterns and other relationships to lay the foundation of algebraic thought. By the end of eighth grade, the standard calls for all students to have a good understanding of algebra. Algebra does include algebraic symbols, but symbol manipulation is not the only skill that this standard requires.

The geometry standard calls for students to understand the properties of two and three-dimensional geometric shapes; to work with coordinate geometry and transformational geometry; and to be able to reason geometrically. The standard says that geometry should be learned through concrete models, drawings, or by using computer software.

The measurement standard includes understanding how to give a numeric value to characteristics of an object. Problem-solving with areas and volumes are also included.

The data analysis and probability standard calls for collecting, organizing, and displaying data, using statistical methods to analyze data, making inferences about data, and applying basic concepts of probability.

The problem-solving, reasoning and proof, communication, and connections standards all call for the same ideas as they did in the 1989 version. The call for conceptual understanding continues. The representation standard calls for students to be able to represent their ideas. These representations might include symbols, diagrams, graphs, tables, figures, drawings, and pictures. The emphasis under representation is to include more representations than symbols. Again, in algebra, instead of just using an equation, one could examine the graph or a table of values.

The 2000 standards shift from the 1989 standards in their approach to basic and procedural skills. Although the 2000 standards continue to prefer conceptual approaches to procedural, in numerous places the 2000 standards emphasize that basic skills are important. They state that "A major goal in the early grades . . . is the development of computational fluency with whole numbers."[7] However, the 2000 standards continue to state that the remaining ideas (their process standards and the new content, such as discrete mathematics, probability, and statistics) are equally important. Although the 2000 standards are now stating that basic skills are needed, the standards do not go so far as to explain how to achieve everything that is now demanded. In other words, the 1989 standards introduced a considerable amount of new content and processes into mathematics. To make space for the new, basic skills, computations and procedures were to be deemphasized. The 2000 standards do not go so far as to say to emphasize those things again, but do state that those things matter (and by reading between the lines, one could say that they have withdrawn their recommendation to deemphasize them). However, how a teacher will make time for everything is anyone's guess. Since the new is still more valued, the 2000 standards continue to imply that basic skills should get the short end of the stick.

That technology "should be an integral part of mathematics education in school" has not changed from the 1989 to the 2000 edition.[8] However, the 2000 standards call for technology not to replace basic skills, but to "foster" basic skills.[9] Again, we see a backing off of statements made in 1989, and yet it is difficult to say how this will play out.

The 1989 standards also called for a deemphasis of algebra. Again, the 2000 standards back off some. They indicate that all students should have a solid background in algebra. Symbol manipulation is important, but they reiterate that other representations matter as well (such as solving an algebraic equation graphically). In the 2000 standards, rather than in 1989 when symbol manipulation was decreased to make room for the new ideas, no suggestion is given for how to make time for it all.

The biggest difference between the 1989 and 2000 set of standards is that many of the previous suggestions for decreased attention to basic skills, computations, and procedures have been removed. Specific statements of the importance of these skills are in place in the 2000 standards, although they are certainly not emphasized to the degree that other content and processes are, nor to the degree that mathematicians would like to see them emphasized. The additions from the 1989 standards are still in place. No suggestions are made as to what can be done to include everything in one mathematics curriculum. Although the NCTM-oriented side can truthfully say that in their 2000 standards they have put back in what was taken out in the 1989 standards, the traditional side says that the whole truth has not been told. A simplification of what has happened is this: the 1989 standards came under criticism for leaving important things out, so those things were put back in. However, they were listed last on a ranked order list of importance, and there is really little possibility of curricula being able to get to everything on the list.

The important thing, then, is how all this plays out in curricula, not how all this plays out in the standards documents. How it is currently playing out in NCTM-oriented curricula is the topic of the next chapter.

SUMMARY

The National Council of Teachers of Mathematics (NCTM) has written and disseminated four sets of standards. In these standards, the NCTM lays out radically different mathematics curricula and pedagogy from traditional curricula and pedagogy. The 1989 standards introduce new content as well as new processes. Since the new will take time, the 1989 standards delineate areas in which decreased attention can be given. These areas include basic computational skills as well as by-hand symbol manipulation. The 2000 standards back off from saying that it is acceptable to give decreased attention to these areas. However, the 2000 standards still call for increased attention to other areas. The 2000 standards do not explain how curricula will allow for everything.

CHAPTER 7

What Distinguishes NCTM-Oriented Curricula?

The previous six chapters have given information on what has happened "behind the scenes" in mathematics education. Eventually as a teacher, one shuts the door and teaches. Despite philosophies, research, conferences, and all the other things that go on, the bottom line is students in a classroom and teachers teaching. The question of interest is: How are teachers teaching?

Teachers follow the adopted textbook. Teachers are too busy to develop their own curriculum. And even if they did have time, they are under too many constraints. They have to meet state standards and testing schedules, and the textbook is picked to accommodate. Textbooks are not usually picked by teachers, but by administrators or mathematics specialists. These people tend to support the National Council of Teachers of Mathematics (NCTM). This is how NCTM-oriented curricula end up in schools. Also, there are some states that, because of their size, practically have the power to set a national mathematics curriculum. These states include Texas, California, and New York. For this reason, the math wars originated in California.

Textbooks are important. Knowing that textbooks are important, NCTM worked to gain the support of the National Science Foundation (NSF). The NCTM was successful in that endeavor. The NSF advertised grant opportunities for mathematics educators who wanted to develop a mathematics curriculum in alignment with NCTM standards (the previous chapter in this book described those standards). The results of these projects are the NCTM-oriented curricula.

There are NCTM-oriented curricula that were developed independently of NSF funds as well. And again, in order to be adopted, a curriculum is going to claim to be NCTM-oriented. However, those that created the math wars are from the set that was originally developed under NSF funds.

Examples of NCTM-oriented curricula at the elementary level include *Math Trailblazers* (Teaching Integrated Math and Science), *Everyday Mathematics* (University of Chicago School Mathematics Project Elementary), and *Investigations in Number, Data, and Space* (the Technical Education Research Center, or TERC). Examples at the middle school level include *Connected Mathematics* (Connected Mathematics Project), *Mathematics in Context* (the development of an "achieved" curriculum for middle school), *MATH Thematics* (Six through Eight Mathematics), *Pathways to Algebra and Geometry* (Middle School Mathematics through Applications Project), and *MathScape* (Seeing and Thinking Mathematically). Examples at the high school level include *Contemporary Mathematics in Context* (Core Plus Mathematics Project), *Interactive Mathematics Program* (IMP), *MATH Connections* (Secondary Mathematics Core Curriculum Initiative), *SIMMS Integrated Mathematics: A Modeling Approach Using Technology* (Systemic Initiative for Montana Mathematics and Science: Integrated Mathematics Project), *Mathematics: Modeling Our World* (Applications/Reform in Secondary Education), and *Connected Geometry*. The University of Chicago School Mathematics Project Secondary Component is for both middle and high school and is a series of textbooks (*Transition Mathematics* is one of them). Rather than give details on each of these curriculum, I will give details on one from each of the levels (elementary, middle, and high school) and then give the main characteristics of the NCTM-oriented curricula.

AN ELEMENTARY CURRICULUM

Let us turn first to a specific elementary curriculum, *Math Trailblazers*.[1] *Math Trailblazers* is a K–5 curriculum with six mathematical content strands: number and operation; geometry and spatial sense; measurement; data analysis, statistics, and probability; fractions and decimals;

and, patterns, functions, and algebra. In addition, a minimum of eight special labs per year are incorporated in the curriculum. These labs are investigations into some mathematical content (for example, classification, length, area, volume, and mass).

An example lesson from second grade is "marshmallows and containers." In this lesson, students work with the concept of volume. Students are given marshmallows and three different containers. They are asked how to find out which container can hold the most marshmallows. Students can fill each of the containers and then count the marshmallows. However, when they are counting the marshmallows, they are shown how to count by tens (with leftovers). In this way, they are taught principles of grouping and the base-10 system. The results from their experiments are recorded in a data table, graphed, and then analyzed to formulate conclusions. Additional questions (for example, how many total marshmallows did you use?) allow the students to practice arithmetic.

Math Trailblazers uses the approach of posing questions that allow students to use concrete materials to investigate mathematical content. Students are required to both find solutions and explain all answers and processes to their classmates. Solutions are represented through a variety of methods (examples include number sentences, graphs, pictures, and charts). The concrete materials are from students' everyday lives (examples include egg cartons, marshmallows, and water).

A MIDDLE SCHOOL CURRICULUM

Let us turn to a specific middle school curriculum, *Connected Mathematics*,[2] a mathematics curriculum for grades six through eight with special attention paid to the NCTM standard for connections. *Connected Mathematics* strives to make explicit the connections between mathematical topics, between school mathematics and everyday mathematics, and between what a middle-schooler cares about and the topics of mathematics. Each year of the curriculum consists of eight modules. The modules cover such content as number, geometry, measurement, algebra, probability, and statistics. The curriculum contains problem settings that require groups of students to work with mathematics, to be involved in discussions, and to do writing.

Students learn about algebra. They often solve the problems using their graphing calculators. The algebra learning is embedded in the story problems. Students are asked to describe patterns (what is similar and what is different), and then make predications by using the patterns. (This is a very different algebra than the paper-and-pencil symbol manipulation found in traditional mathematics.) Connections between equations, tables, and graphs are also emphasized.

Day-to-day lessons follow a three-step process. The teacher *launches* the lesson (sets up the context and the mathematical question). Students *explore* (the teacher walks around the room as a facilitator). At the end, the teacher leads the *summary* class discussion. This pattern of launch, explore, and summary is repeated throughout the year.

Connected Mathematics makes heavy use of calculators, following the philosophy that calculators should always be available. Graphing calculators are used beginning in the seventh grade. In the sixth grade, students use nongraphing calculators. Calculators are used for solving complicated computations and equations, among other uses.

In *Connected Mathematics*, students learn mathematics by working problems, and not by listening to a lecture. Students reflect on problems and solutions and communicate with each other. All problems have a variety of solutions.

An example problem involves a pizzeria. Students must measure circles, and are hopefully inclined to look for a formula for finding circumference and area. Students create tables with circle measurements (radius, diameter, circumference, and area) as well as determine the price of each pizza. Using tables and graphs, the students can narrow in on a formula for circumference. Perhaps they will say, "Circumference is the diameter times a little more than 3." The teacher will then help with the concept of pi. A similar process is followed to learn the area of a circle.

This example demonstrates well the *Connected Mathematics* curriculum. In traditional curricula, students are told the formulas for circumference and area. Although teachers may try to justify the formulas, students do not "discover" them in traditional curricula. In *Connected Mathematics*, students discover them. Of course, this is a time-consuming process. Yet, it is certainly true that one tends to remember what one discovers for oneself. (This last sentence is not intended to imply that discovery is the *only* method by which students tend to remember something.)

A HIGH SCHOOL CURRICULUM

This brings us to the high school curriculum that we will examine, *Contemporary Mathematics in Context*, better known as Core Plus.[3] Core Plus is a three-year high school mathematics curriculum for all students, with a fourth-year course for college-bound students. The main theme of Core Plus is mathematics as sense-making. Students investigate problems set in real-life contexts within an integrated curriculum that includes algebra and functions, geometry and trigonometry, statistics and probability, and discrete mathematics. This means that there are no isolated courses (algebra, geometry, trigonometry, etc.), but three (or four) years of Core Plus, each year having a little of each topic. By the end of the three (or four) years, the students will have all the material.

The curriculum for each year is seven units and a capstone section, which is "a thematic two-week, project-oriented activity that enables students to pull together and apply the important mathematical concepts and methods developed in the entire course."[4] Mathematical modeling is emphasized throughout the curriculum. Graphing calculators are used. Additional characteristics of Core Plus are that the curriculum is designed to be accessible to all students, to engage the students in active learning, and to provide multidimensional assessment. The assessments are embedded within the curriculum and include students' answers to questions in class, groupwork, student journals, quizzes, in-class and take-home end-of-unit assessments, cumulative written assessments, and extended projects.

Inclusion of topics in the Core Plus curriculum is based on the merits of the topics themselves; that is, the topics must be important in their own right. This means there is no mathematics for mathematics' sake in the curriculum. The instructional sequence follows a four-step process labeled as launch, explore, share and summarize, and apply. The "launch" sets the context for what is to follow and consists of a class discussion of a problem. The "explore" is usually a cooperative group or pair activity in which students investigate the problems and questions. "Share and summarize" brings the class back together to discuss key concepts and methods. "Apply" is time in which individual students practice what has been learned.

An example lesson is difficult to provide for Core Plus because of the length and complexity of the lessons. I will give a short description of three different lessons, without giving the details. One content area is exponential growth. The lesson is launched by describing a situation in which a sewage spill has polluted natural waters (for example, lakes). The cleanup procedure takes time. Graphs of the amount left to be cleaned up versus time are given. Students are asked questions that can be answered by interpreting the graphs.

Another lesson, this one from the geometry strand, has content about right angles and similarity. In this lesson, two school crossing signs are shown, one smaller than the other. The signs are similar. (Similar is a mathematical term, and not used in the sense of day-to-day similar or alike.) Questions ask the students to draw triangles that are similar to each other.

The last lesson I will describe has the definition of a fair price for a game. This is the price that should be charged so that the players break even in the long run. Various games are described, and the students are to find the fair price.

THE AVERAGE NCTM-ORIENTED CURRICULUM

We have briefly looked at three curricula, one each for elementary, middle, and high school students. Rather than examine further examples of NCTM-oriented curricula, we will now consider main characteristics. Although any one curriculum may not have every single characteristic, we will still be able to paint a picture of an "average" curriculum that is NCTM-oriented. It is important to understand that NCTM-oriented curricula differ from traditional curricula in substantial manners. For that reason, while describing the NCTM-oriented curricula, I will also try to give comparisons to traditional.

Calculators are used extensively in NCTM-oriented curricula. The use of technology, in particular calculators, is very different between NCTM-oriented and traditional. Traditional curricula make very little use of calculators, with almost no use at the elementary and middle school levels. At the high school level, traditional curricula will bring in calculators at certain points in time. On the other side are NCTM-oriented curricula, which make use of calculators constantly. Beginning in the earliest grades, students use four-function calculators (four-function calculators mean that the calculator is able to add, subtract, multiply, and divide). In middle and high school, students use calculators that graph and do algebra.

By using calculators, students can quickly move between representations of the same situation (for example, examine a graph, solve an equation, and look for patterns in a table). This process builds understanding. However, the calculator is also used to replace skills that students once learned to do by hand. Supporters of calculator use argue two different things. First, they claim that research supports that students will learn basic facts despite using a calculator. Second, they argue that even if a student does not learn how to do procedures by hand, there will always be calculators. They ask, if a calculator replaces basic skills, so what? Because the students are doing higher mathematics than they would be able to do if they were stuck in the basic skills, it is fine if they cannot do basic skills. Arguing that a student should know how to do everything by hand is like arguing that a farmer should make sure he knows how to do everything without equipment. If the equipment broke down, wouldn't the farmer have it repaired? The same argument, NCTM says, holds for calculators.

Opponents of calculator use also argue two things. First, they argue that the calculator is replacing basic arithmetic facts as well as algebraic skills. They argue that students are not going to learn how to do something that calculators can do for them. They compare the calculator to a "black box" in which students enter numbers and the answer comes out. They argue that using calculators does not build number sense. (Number sense is difficult to describe. It is a "feel" for numbers. If someone has number sense, they will be able to know when the clerk has rung something up incorrectly. They will have a sense of what the total bill ought to be.) Second, they argue that knowing how to do the basics by hand is what lays a foundation for true understanding of higher concepts. Knowing how to do basic arithmetic is important for understanding the entire mathematical system. Some also argue that mathematics has always been a disciplined study, and if we remove the practice and rote nature of parts of mathematics, we have lost something. We have lost the ability of the study of mathematics to build the person into a good student and a good thinker.

Both sides agree that with calculators, a student can do more "complicated" problems, which might just mean problems with messy numbers. These numbers might be realistic. However, the sides disagree over whether realistic is an important thing or not. The traditional side simply does not mind if the numbers in problems need to be made "easy" so that students can do the problems by hand. The NCTM-oriented side has the advantage of being able to claim that the problems could actually occur in life.

An additional concern about calculators is that the colleges are still expecting incoming students to be able to do high school mathematics by hand and not be dependent on a calculator. Colleges will place incoming students into mathematics courses that the students have already had, because the students cannot demonstrate their knowledge without a calculator. The NCTM-oriented side's response is that they are interested in more students than just the college-bound, and, anyway, the college-bound should be able to pick up the skills quickly.

This discussion leads into the next difference between the two sets of curricula. The NCTM-oriented curricula put much less emphasis on basic skills and algebraic skills than the traditional do. The arguments on both sides are the same as with the use of calculators. Suffice to explain what this looks like in curricula. In mathematics, there are certain algorithms. These are step-by-step procedures for solving certain types of problems. It is easy to build into a calculator the steps necessary to perform these procedures. In NCTM-oriented curricula, the students are shown how to use calculators to perform these algorithms. Compare this to traditional curricula, which show students how to do these procedures by hand.

A similar situation exists with algebra. Traditional algebra consists of solving equations symbolically. Equations in algebra usually have a variable (or an unknown; these are the x's you might remember), numbers, and an equal sign (there are numbers and/or variables on both sides of the equal sign). In traditional algebra, students are taught how to "solve" these equations; that is, how to figure out what x is. They are taught various algorithms for moving the numbers and symbols around, isolating x, and thus finding out what x is. The NCTM-oriented supporters call that "meaningless symbol pushing" and argue that none of it is taught in such a manner so that how to solve equations makes any sense to students. Rather, students just push symbols around.

In the NCTM-oriented curricula, much less attention is given to symbol manipulation. Rather, equations are graphed (using the graphing calculator) and/or a table of values is found (using a built-in table function in the graphing calculator) and students can find out what x is, if in fact they need to know what x is. In general, students do not practice finding x; they find x if it is important for whatever else they are learning at the time. This is not to say that students never solve an algebraic equation in the traditional fashion. Sometimes they do, and sometimes textbooks are supplemented with exercises that have them do so. However, the quantity of time spent on this is considerably less than in traditional curricula. The argument is that the process that is replacing the symbol manipulation is better because it is "sense-making," and the student can better understand what the equation means. When NCTM-oriented people talk about sense-making, they are first complaining that traditional curricula tell how to do something, but not why it works. Thus, students do not make sense of what they are doing. The NCTM-oriented curricula present methods for which the "why" is built into the process. For example, when x is zero in an equation, it might represent a real-life situation about which students can think. Or, if the equation represents a cost function, zero could be the cost of producing no items. The argument is that mathematics makes sense when methods other than symbol-pushing are used.

Besides a deemphasis on certain content, some of the NCTM-oriented curricula are integrated in their content. This is commonly confused to mean that other subjects (such as science) are mixed in with mathematics. Actually, integrated refers to topics within mathematics. In traditional curricula, the various topics in mathematics are taught as separate courses (for example, algebra is a separate course from geometry). In integrated courses, some of each of the usually separate courses are taught every year. In theory, at the end of a three-year sequence, students have the full year of each course (one-third of each course is taught in each of the three years). "In theory" is used for two reasons. First, the NCTM-oriented curricula do not want to cover the complete courses (as they want to make room for other topics). Second, traditional supporters argue that by the time students are catching on to some topic, the curriculum moves on to another topic. Then, when the curriculum returns to the topic, so much time has passed that the teacher has to start over. Thus, the material takes much longer to cover than in nonintegrated courses, and enough material is not covered for students to receive the equivalent of each course. The NCTM-oriented people argue that integrated courses result in a more natural manner in which to teach mathematics and show the connections.

We have spent a lot of time on content that is deemphasized in NCTM-oriented curricula. The flip side is that the NCTM-oriented curricula have content that traditional curricula do not. This content includes discrete mathematics, probability, and statistics, which are used in computer science and data analysis. Because the world has turned very data-driven, it is argued that the content is important for school mathematics. Opponents are not against the content, but concerned that it takes up time. Thus, the traditional content is then shortchanged, while the new content could be covered in college. In addition, opponents do not believe that the discrete mathematics is actually useful in everyday life and can be learned in college if it is needed for college. Further, the low level at which the topics must be taught at a K–12 grade level is too low to really help students. Again, the argument is to just leave statistics, probability, and discrete mathematics for college. The NCTM-oriented people disagree with all the opponents' arguments, except they agree that covering discrete mathematics, probability, and statistics takes up time. However, NCTM supporters argue that it is fine that it takes up time. Besides, they argue, not all students go to college.

Other than different content, the manner in which the content is presented is quite different. The NCTM-oriented curricula require different pedagogical techniques from the teacher than traditional curricula require. The NCTM-oriented curricula are designed for group work and group discussions. Traditional curricula have students working as individuals and listening to the teacher. Instead of exercises (common in traditional), NCTM-oriented curricula are heavy on group problem-solving and investigations. The curricula are often set up so that the teacher introduces a topic and then students are responsible for working with each other to conduct experiments and make conjectures. The teacher is responsible for leading the conclusion or summary session at the end. During investigation times, students are sometimes responsible for inventing algorithms. Traditional curricula will tell students the standard algorithms and have students practice. Telling students the standard algorithms saves time. The NCTM-oriented manner is better for students' remembering. What we discover for ourselves is easier to remember than what someone tells us. The NCTM-oriented curricula stress that students must *understand* what they do and learn conceptually. Traditional curricula emphasis on procedures sometimes causes the conceptual understanding to be lost. (By the way, teaching as a facilitator is more difficult than teaching as a teller. As a facilitator, the teacher gives up control and may be caught not knowing an answer.)

Besides content, there are the processes of problem-solving, communication, representation, reasoning, and connections. These processes are present as supplementary material (or not present at all) in traditional curricula. The NCTM-oriented curricula have many opportunities for these processes to take place. The communication comes with the discussions and group work. Representation occurs with the use of graphing calculators to form graphs and tables. Connections occur through the integrated nature of the curricula as well as through real-life examples. I will say a little more about problem-solving and reasoning.

The NCTM-oriented curricula contain lots of problems set in real-life contexts. Traditional curricula have lots of problems without a context at all. The two different kinds of curricula (NCTM-oriented versus traditional) look very different in this particular area. The NCTM-oriented do not contain mathematics for mathematics' sake. If the mathematics is not part of an application, it is not covered. The next chapter in this book gives more details on how NCTM-oriented curricula and traditional curricula differ in their approaches to problem-solving.

The NCTM-oriented curricula do much more with justifications of mathematical principles, but much less with formal proofs than the traditional curricula. Mathematicians appreciate proofs, but NCTM-oriented supporters argue that it is more important that students are able to understand. It is indeed debatable what level of mathematical proof is understandable to students at the K–12 level.

There is another difference worth mentioning. The NCTM-oriented curricula do not track. All students are in the same classes. Traditional curricula often have separate tracks for students (depending on if the students are college-bound or how well the students have done in mathematics courses in the past).

In summary, there are many differences between NCTM-oriented and traditional curricula. Here is an oversimplification, but hopefully a helpful one. Traditional and NCTM-oriented have chunks of curricula switched. What traditional is all about, NCTM-oriented considers supplementary. And what NCTM-oriented is all about, traditional considers supplementary. Deciding which side to be on is a matter of what one values. Of course, this is a nice place for me to mention again that finding a balance between the two might be ideal. This balance is difficult to achieve and has not yet been achieved.

The NCTM-oriented curricula are for K–12 grades. Although not everyone goes on to college, a lot of students do. In chapter 9 we will briefly examine mathematics teaching and learning at the college level, including how future mathematics teachers are taught. However, we will spend the bulk of the chapter examining the transition between secondary mathematics and college mathematics. One of the largest concerns in the math wars is how students in NCTM-oriented curricula do once they get to college. Based on this chapter's discussion of NCTM-oriented curricula, you might realize that much of what college mathematics professors want students to be able to do is not at the heart of NCTM-oriented curricula.

SUMMARY

The NCTM-oriented curricula differ from traditional curricula in substantial manners. The NCTM-oriented curricula do not promote any particular mathematics content, but prefer that students learn how to think mathematically. Technology use is extensive. The NCTM-oriented curricula involve many opportunities for students to work in groups, discuss mathematics, and grapple with open-ended problems. Real-life data and mathematical modeling are often present in NCTM-oriented curricula. Some traditional procedures are absent from NCTM-oriented curricula, and the emphasis on basic skills and by-hand symbol manipulation (algebra) is much lighter in NCTM-oriented curricula than in traditional curricula.

CHAPTER 8

What Distinguishes NCTM-Oriented Problems from Traditional Problems?

As the last chapter described, numerous differences exist between NCTM-oriented curricula and traditional curricula. One of the most important differences is found in the nature of the mathematics problems found in NCTM-oriented curricula and traditional curricula. This chapter describes five themes that occur when problems from each type of curriculum are compared and illustrates the themes by giving examples of problems from each type of curriculum. The NCTM-oriented problems differ from traditional problems in at least the following manners. The NCTM-oriented problems use real-life data, tend to be open-ended, are not exercises, are nonroutine, and are conceptual. On the other hand, traditional problems use contrived data, lend themselves to one answer, are often exercises, are routine, and are procedural.

A disclaimer is necessary before describing each of these themes. Traditional curricula follow the philosophy that problems assigned to students should start simple and build to more complex. As the complexity level of the problems build, the quantity of the problems decreases. Thus, it is true that traditional curricula contain many more procedural problems (which are simpler) than conceptual problems (which are more difficult). But, it is not true that conceptual problems are absent from traditional curricula. Of course, a teacher is free to spend the bulk of time on the earlier problems in a textbook section, and this often happens.

The NCTM-oriented curricula tend to follow a different philosophy than starting with simple problems and building up to more difficult problems. Problems in NCTM-oriented curricula tend to be in the middle level of difficulty. There are very, very few simple, procedural problems.

When the reader reads this chapter on problems in NCTM-oriented curricula versus traditional curricula, please keep in mind that I am describing the typical or average problem found in these two types of curriculum. Thus, the NCTM-oriented problems, which tend to be in the middle level of difficulty, will appear to be considerably "better" than the traditional approach, which have many more problems at the simple level. The reader may still reasonably conclude that the NCTM-oriented version of problems is better than the traditional version of problems. Yet, it is important to understand why traditional curricula value the problems that they do value; that is, traditional curricula contain these simple problems for pedagogical reasons.

REAL-LIFE DATA VERSUS CONTRIVED DATA

Because NCTM-oriented curricula allow and even depend on technology (that is, calculators), numbers used in the problems can be "difficult" numbers. Difficult might mean that the numbers involve decimals. Easy numbers are those whole numbers whose involved calculations are easy. For example, if a problem calls for division, then those whole numbers that will result in whole-number division are used to make a problem easy. If there is not a desire to make the problem easy, then any numbers will do. For example, 12 divided by 3 is easy; 12 divided by 5 is harder; and 12.543 divided by 2.3671 is difficult. In trigonometry, certain angles (such as 30, 45, 60, and 90-degree angles) are easier to work with than other angles (such as 33 or 77 degrees). If students are not allowed calculators, trigonometry curricula must either use the easier angles or provide tables of values. Compare the following two problems.

> *One:* Joan has $23\frac{1}{3}$ yards of material with which to make shirts. Each shirt uses $2\frac{1}{6}$ yards. How many complete shirts can she make?
>
> *Two:* Joan has 24 yards of material with which to make shirts. Each shirt uses 3 yards of material. How many complete shirts can she make?

Both problems require an identical mathematical process, division. Problem one requires a more difficult division calculation than problem two does. If the purpose of the problem is to see if students know what to do (and not necessarily know how to do the division), then it doesn't matter if the division is easy or hard. Yet, if the division is difficult, it might prevent the student from completing the problem. Traditional curricula avoid the issue by using easy numbers, resulting in an easy division. The NCTM-oriented curricula will use the "messier" numbers, but allow the use of calculators. Many calculators even allow students to input fractions exactly as they appear in the problem. With certain calculators, then, solving problem one is a matter of two things: knowing that it involves division, and knowing how to use the calculator to perform division. The second problem involves knowing that the problem involves division, and knowing how to carry out a basic division (24 divided by 3).

The traditional curricula philosophy is that both knowing to divide and being able to divide are important. Further, traditional supporters will argue that all problems in K–12 curricula are contrived; none are real-life problems. The argument is that real-life problems are way too messy for K–12 curricula, and even NCTM-oriented curricula use contrived problems that are set in a somewhat real-life setting.

The NCTM-oriented philosophy is that it is more likely that the first problem would be a problem in everyday life than the second problem. Therefore, it is important that students know what mathematical process is needed to solve the problem (that is, they know that division is needed), but it is not important that they can do the division without the aid of a calculator. Further, if students practice on problems that are more likely to occur in real life, there is a better chance that their school mathematics ability will transfer to real-life mathematics ability.

OPEN-ENDED PROBLEMS VERSUS ONE-ANSWER PROBLEMS

Sometimes the term "open-ended" is used to simply mean problems that are not multiple-choice in format. However, open-ended more often means that the problems lend themselves to many different solution processes, and there is neither one right solution process nor one right final answer. Answers to open-ended problems might be a paragraph of English words that will vary by student. One-answer problems are problems that *intend* the student to find the one correct solution process for solving the problem, and that solution process leads to one correct final answer, which is an exact numeric answer. (This "one answer" may consist of several numbers. For example, the solution set to a quadratic equation may contain two numbers. This is still *one* correct answer.) Note that an emphasis was placed on the word "intend" in the previous sentence, because it is almost always possible to find more than one solution path in any mathematical problem. However, the problems in traditional mathematics are intended to teach (and later have students practice) a *particular* solution path, and therefore are designed to lend themselves to that particular solution path. Traditional mathematics curricula tend to have one-answer problems, and NCTM-oriented curricula tend to have open-ended problems.

Consider the following two problems. The first is open-ended, and the second is not.

> *One:* Lily decides to set up a lemonade stand. She has two types of lemonade, one that costs 15¢ a cup to make and another that costs 5¢ a cup to make. What should Lily consider in trying to set up the best lemonade stand?
>
> *Two:* Lily decides to set up a lemonade stand. She has two types of lemonade, one that costs 15¢ a cup to make and another that costs 5¢ a cup to make. She decides to mix 1/3 of the 15¢ a cup lemonade with 2/3 of the 5¢ a cup lemonade. How much should she charge for each cup of the mixed lemonade?

The first problem has no *one* solution to it; it has many solutions. The solutions are not simply numeric answers, either. The first problem is rich in mathematical possibilities. For example, students might discuss how it would be best to mix the two types of lemonade, in order to charge a reasonable price and still have quality lemonade. In other words, it is possible that the students will turn the first problem into a version of the second problem. Note that the first problem is also rich in nonmathematical possibilities, and it is the teacher's job to keep the problem centered on mathematics. (In fact, mathematicians will argue that it is not a well-defined question because what makes lemonade "best" is not a mathematical question. What makes lemonade best is an experimental question, according to mathematicians.)

Setting aside mathematicians' objections, let us pretend that NCTM-oriented students decide to turn the first problem into the second problem. There are then many additional directions that the students can take the first problem after they are done with the first direction. For example, the students might ask how much of the lemonade they have (it is unlikely that there is a limitless supply). Based on how much lemonade they have, how much of each type (the 15¢ and 5¢ type) should they make? This is a different mathematics question. There are many other mathematics questions possible from Lily's lemonade stand under version one of the problem.

The second problem has only one possible direction. The second problem is a routine mathematics question. It is a word problem of the type called "product-mix." There is a mathematical procedure that will solve the problem. Once the mathematical procedure is correctly applied, all students will end up with the same (one correct) numeric answer. Again, there is basically one correct intended solution path (applying the intended procedure), although it is certainly possible to solve the problem in a variety of manners.

The first problem is more likely to occur in NCTM-oriented curricula, and the second problem in traditional curricula. But, recall that the first problem could be turned into the second. This is a good example of the fact that NCTM-oriented problems (open-ended problems) may certainly end up including a lot of traditional mathematics, but not because the NCTM-oriented problems were specifically designed to include particular mathematics. The NCTM-oriented curricula include mathematics that "happen" to arise out of the open-ended problems. If a particular teacher really valued product-mix problems, she might make sure that the students end up asking the second question about Lily's lemonade stand. If a teacher thought that product-mix problems are not all that important, that teacher may take the first problem in a completely different direction than problem two. Either way, some good mathematics would be done. Therefore, any one open-ended problem may or may not end up including some traditional mathematics content and procedures. (This is what is meant by not including mathematics just for mathematics' sake, but including that mathematics that arises out of situations.)

The NCTM-oriented curricula spend a lot of time on one problem, because the problems are open-ended and lead to numerous explorations. The traditional curricula state the problems as they want the problems explored, and thus any one problem does not lead to numerous explorations.

Open-ended problems occur often in NCTM-oriented curricula and are especially used to introduce new topics in NCTM-oriented curricula. For example, one mathematical topic present in some NCTM-oriented curricula and absent from traditional curricula is how to devise a voting system that is ethical. It is possible, when there are more than two candidates running for an office, that plurality voting is quite unfair. A candidate who would have beaten each of the other candidates in a head-to-head election might lose under plurality voting. An open-ended problem that NCTM-oriented curricula might use follows.

> *Open-ended problem:* Five students are running for class president. Every high school student has a right to vote. Devise at least two methods for deciding the winner of the election and explain manners in which each method is fair and unfair to the candidates.

After students explore this problem for, say, a class period, the teacher might explain various voting algorithms that mathematicians have created. Or, a teacher might simply explore the algorithms that students invent. In traditional curricula, this particular topic would not be covered, but if it were, the algorithms would simply be presented and students would practice them. In traditional curricula, students would not invent their own algorithms.

NONROUTINE VERSUS ROUTINE

Routine problems are those for which a procedural process should be applied. The purpose of routine problems is for students to think of the routine procedure that ought to be applied, and then gain practice by applying it. Nonroutine problems do not easily lend themselves to a procedural solution. With nonroutine problems, each problem is unique and requires a different approach. The purpose of nonroutine problems is to place students in a situation in which they have to think mathematically, and then gain proficiency at mathematical thinking through repeated situations. Traditional curricula have routine problems, and NCTM-oriented curricula prefer nonroutine problems.

Lily's lemonade stand under the second wording is a routine problem. Here is another example of a routine problem.

A routine problem: Tom has 10 coins in his pocket, all nickels and pennies, for a total of 38¢. How many nickels are in his pocket?

The solution path is algebraic. The student should form two equations as follow:

$$N + P = 10$$
$$.05N + .01P = .38$$

The first equation represents that the total number of nickels plus the total number of pennies is 10, the number of coins in Tom's pocket. The second equation represents that the total amount of cents contributed by the nickels is 5¢ times the number of nickels, and the pennies contribute one cent each, and this must sum to 38¢. (The second equation could be written: $5N + P = 38$.) By solving these equations algebraically, the student would figure out that there have to be 7 nickels and 3 pennies in Tom's pocket.

The NCTM-oriented curricula would define Tom's coins as a routine problem, and thus solving it is not problem-solving. At best, solving that problem is an exercise (more about exercises versus problems below). The NCTM standards believe that working on such problems is not worth the time. Although mathematicians are not so interested in how many coins are in Tom's pocket, mathematicians do like the algebraic process that occurs in solving the problem and would label the process as problem-solving. The purpose of solving a problem like Tom's coins is to give students practice at algebraic solution processes. If students solve Tom's coins problem and many others like it, they will become proficient at algebra. It is difficult to become proficient at nonroutine problems, because there is no repeated practice (if the problems are repeated, they would become routine). However, it is still hoped by NCTM-oriented supporters that students will become more able to think mathematically by solving many nonroutine problems.

If NCTM-oriented curricula contained a problem like Tom's coins (which is unlikely), it might be suggested that students find several different solution strategies for solving the problem. A student could reason this way:

> Tom could have 0 nickels and 10 pennies, does that total 38¢?
> Tom could have 1 nickel and 9 pennies, does that total 38¢?
> Tom could have 2 nickels and 8 pennies, does that total 38¢?

In this manner the student could go through the possibilities and solve the problem while never relying on algebra. A student might even reason this way, "Tom must have at least 3 pennies, because the total is 38¢. So, if I think in sets of five, then there are three pennies left over. With 3 pennies, there are only 7 coins left (out of the 10 in Tom's pocket), so those must be nickels."

The NCTM standards would rate students' thinking as given above as a better mathematical practice than following an algebraic procedure to solve the problem. Therefore, those that support NCTM-oriented curricula might prefer the thought processes just mentioned to the algebraic solution process. In the case of Tom's coins, teachers might show students how to make a table, with a column for the number of pennies, a column for the number of nickels, and a column for the solution to $.05N + .01P$, the total amount of cents in Tom's pocket. Students have found their solution when that sum, $.05N + .01P$, equals 38¢.

Mathematicians would appreciate the student who started listing the possibilities, but then mathematicians would point out that if Tom has 100 coins in his pocket, this method is exhausting. It is much better to use algebra. The last student, the one who thinks the situation through, will also be appreciated by mathematicians, but mathematicians would try to let this student know that his thinking worked in this situation because it was a rather easy problem. Algebra is powerful because solving the situation algebraically is not only efficient, but a sure solution process. Algebra will always work. Traditional supporters would ask: Why have something as powerful as algebra and not use it?

Let us turn now to an example of a nonroutine problem.

> *Nonroutine problem:* Carol Jane prints out a 132-page manuscript and realizes that she has failed to number the pages. Rather than reprint the manuscript, she decides to use a typewriter to type the page numbers on each page of her manuscript. How many keystrokes will this take?

Students do not have a memorized procedure for solving that problem. Students need to think about what the problem is asking, brainstorm on solution methods, try a solution method, and check to see if their solution method worked. In other words, students must do what NCTM-oriented curricula label the "problem-solving process." (If the reader is curious, the answer is 288, because there are 9 pages with single-digit numbers (the numbers 1 through 9), and 90 pages with two-digit numbers (numbers 10 through 99), and 33 pages with three-digit numbers (numbers 100 through 132). Thus, one performs this sum: $9 + 2 \cdot 90 + 3 \cdot 33$, where I have used a dot to represent multiplication.)

NCTM-oriented curricula might contain Carol Jane's problem. Traditional curricula would not, as Carol Jane's problem does not contribute toward practicing mathematical procedures. The problem may contribute toward practicing thinking mathematically. Yet traditional curricula consider solving mathematical procedures to be thinking mathematically, and there is only so much time.

One additional note is important. Whether a problem is routine or nonroutine is a function of the student working the problem. Carol Jane's typewriter problem would be nonroutine to secondary students, but it would be routine to mathematicians. In fact, mathematicians see a procedure for working it (it is a geometric series problem with a remainder term). So, nonroutine does not imply that no routine exists; only that no routine would come to mind to the person working the problem. Traditional supporters would argue that all problems are routine, and this distinction between routine and nonroutine is not an important one.

PROBLEMS VERSUS EXERCISES

The distinction between problems and exercises is similar to the distinction between routine and nonroutine problems. To be considered a problem by NCTM-oriented curricula, the problem must be nonroutine and set in a real-life setting. An exercise is a routine problem with or without a real-life setting, according to NCTM-oriented curricula.

Traditional curricula do not make a distinction between routine and nonroutine. Any problem set in a real-life setting is a problem, according to traditional curricula. In addition, some problems not set in real-life settings are still considered problems by traditional curricula. Traditional curricula may actually call the same items problems and exercises, with the distinction being how often the student has tried the item. If a set of items has been worked many times by students, and then an additional similar set is assigned for practice, those items would then be called exercises by traditional curricula. The NCTM-oriented curricula do not have exercises. The following examples are labeled according to traditional curricula, and with the hopes of clarifying the situation.

An exercise: Factor. $x^2 - 5x + 6$

An exercise: Solve for x. $x^2 - 5x + 6 = 0$

A problem: The height h (in feet) of an object thrown or kicked up in the air can be modeled by a quadratic function, $h(t) = -16t^2 + 2t + 4$, where time is measured in seconds. After 1/2 second, what is the height of the object?

The NCTM-oriented curricula do not have exercises. The two exercises above would either not be in NCTM-oriented curricula or would be set in a setting, as in the example above labeled a problem. The problem would be labeled a routine problem in NCTM-oriented curricula. Routine problems are used in place of exercises and are not a large part of NCTM-oriented curricula. What NCTM-oriented curricula truly label problems (those of a nonroutine nature) are used on a very limited basis in traditional curricula. The bottom line is traditional curricula are heavy on exercises, and NCTM-oriented curricula are heavy on problems.

CONCEPTUAL VERSUS PROCEDURAL

Procedural problems allow students to practice an algorithm that has been taught. Procedural problems are used in traditional curricula. Conceptual problems allow students to explore and think about a situation. Conceptual problems may occur prior to instruction or in place of instruction. In the latter case, teachers act as facilitators of the problem-solving process. Conceptual problems occur in NCTM-oriented curricula. Procedural problems are for drill and practice, while conceptual problems are for learning and deepening understanding. The following examples illustrate the difference between procedural and conceptual problems.

Procedural problem: Computer disks are shipped in boxes of 250. Five boxes arrived at the store, Computer Corner. How many computer disks arrived at Computer Corner?

Conceptual problem: Create a word problem in which multiplication is the solution process.

In the procedural problem, there are two critical steps: deciding to multiply and carrying out the multiplication. In the conceptual problem, students might correctly respond to the problem without ever multiplying. The conceptual problem aims to determine if the student understands the *why* of multiplication, not the *how*. NCTM-oriented curricula are much more centered on the why, because the how could always be done with a calculator. The why cannot be done with a calculator.

The pattern in all five themes is that problems found in traditional curricula require the student to actually perform a mathematical operation or procedure. The problems found in NCTM-oriented curricula require the student to understand a mathematical thought process, but possibly do not require any actual mathematical computation or allow the computations to be done on a calculator. This is another example where requiring both, or finding a balance, would be ideal. However, it is very time-consuming to require all mathematical possibilities. Drilling and practicing by its very nature takes time. Solving conceptual problems also takes a lot of time. Drilling, practicing, and solving conceptual problems probably takes more time than the school year allows.

ALGEBRA

All of the differences mentioned to this point (real-life versus contrived, open-ended versus one answer, problem versus exercise, routine versus nonroutine, conceptual versus procedural) are especially apparent in algebra curricula under NCTM-oriented and under traditional. In fact, algebra is algebraic thinking under NCTM-oriented curricula and is done throughout K–12 grade curricula. Algebra in traditional mathematics curricula occurs as a one- or two-year mathematics course in the middle school and senior high years. In traditional curricula, algebra is a very procedural course, and the main point is to develop advanced symbol manipulation skills, equation-solving skills, and application-solving skills.

Some examples of traditional algebra have already been given. They are repeated here with additional examples.

> Factor. $x^2 - 5x + 6$
>
> Solve for x. $x^2 - 5x + 6 = 0$
>
> Write an expression that expresses the product of the quantity of two times a number taken from six and the quantity of four more than two times the number.
>
> Solve for z. $8z + 6 = z - 2$
>
> Solve for x. $3x < -2 - 2x$
>
> Solve for x. $(4x - 2)^2 = 8$
>
> Solve for x. $x + \sqrt{x - 4} = 4$
>
> Solve for x. $2^x = 8^{x-4}$
>
> Solve for t. $-16t^2 + 24t = 0$

Algebra in NCTM-oriented curricula spends little time on solving equations. The emphasis is on algebraic thinking and algebraic modeling. The algebra is often presented as families of functions. That is, students explore lines, quadratics, exponential, and rational functions, in that order. Instead of solving, as above, students will be given a situation and then be asked to think algebraically about it. An example follows:

> If a gymnast bounces up off a trampoline, her height in feet above the trampoline at any time t seconds might be given by a quadratic function with rule $h(t) = -16t^2 + 24t$. The rule can be used to produce a graph or a table of data describing the gymnast's bounce. At what time does the gymnast return to the trampoline surface?[1]

In the above item, students actually do have to solve an equation, namely $-16t^2 + 24t = 0$. That same equation was listed under traditional curricula, without the context. In addition to the difference in having a context or not, in NCTM-oriented curricula, the students might solve the equation in a different manner than symbol manipulation. Students might use their graphing calculators to graph the equation and then find the intercepts (or roots) of the equation. Or, students might use the table function of their graphing calculators to create a table of values, and narrow in on the answer. The emphasis is moved from symbol manipulation to conceptual understanding. In traditional algebra, the emphasis is on symbol manipulation.

In sum, NCTM-oriented problems tend to have some really nice qualities, such as being nonroutine, not being exercises, being open-ended, using real-life data, and requiring conceptual thought. Traditional problems tend to be the opposite (routine, exercises, one answer, contrived, and procedural). However, traditional supporters argue that these distinctions are not important (for example, all problems are contrived and routine). In addition, traditional supporters argue that they do value and want their problems to have these nice qualities, but it is a matter of what should come first. For students to learn, traditional supporters argue, students must start with lower-level problems and then work their way up to higher levels.

SUMMARY

Solving problems is a major part of mathematics education. However, the nature of the problems differ between NCTM-oriented and traditional curricula. The NCTM-oriented problems are more likely to be nonroutine, be true problems, be open-ended, be set in the context of real-life data, and require conceptual thought. The traditional problems are more likely to be routine, be exercises, not be open-ended, not be set in a context, and require procedural thought. The differences in the nature of the problems between NCTM-oriented and traditional curricula show up especially strong in algebra curricula. Mathematicians especially value algebra.

CHAPTER 9

What Happens to Students as They Reach the College Level?

With the exception of a few comments, the previous chapters have concerned the teaching and learning of K–12 grade students. No picture of college-level mathematics teaching and learning has been painted, although what mathematics professors think of NCTM-oriented curricula, and why they side with traditional curricula, has been covered quite a bit. However, the subset of mathematics professors discussed so far is a rather small subset of all mathematicians. It is not that a larger subset of mathematics professors supports the NCTM-oriented curricula. In fact, very few mathematics professors support it. But, even this is misleading. Most mathematics professors have never heard of NCTM-oriented curricula, nor are they interested in hearing about it.

Mathematics professors have doctorates in mathematics. Almost no mathematics doctoral programs include education courses. Mathematics professors learn how to teach by actually teaching. This is why some mathematics professors are not very good at teaching. Teaching ability is not inborn or an ability that one can "pick up" in time. It is not only possible to teach someone how to teach, it is necessary to teach someone how to teach. While teaching at the K–12 level requires a teaching license, there is no equivalent to a teaching license for postsecondary teaching. Positions in mathematics departments require a graduate degree in mathematics (or something very similar), and that is it.

However, mathematics professors do care about teaching, and mathematics departments would like to hire professors who will be good at teaching. Still, not many professors or mathematics departments are interested in K–12 mathematics teaching and learning. (Of course, the subset of the faculty that deals with educating future teachers is interested.) Many mathematics professors will notice what skills students have upon entering college. But, that interest does not carry over into studying mathematics education at the K–12 level.

This means that NCTM does not have influence on college mathematics education. There is no equivalent to NCTM-oriented curricula at the college level. Mathematics education at the college level resembles traditional mathematics education at the K–12 level. Most mathematicians believe in traditional mathematics skills. Most college mathematics courses require students to be able to "do" mathematics, whether or not the problems are set in real-life settings. Of course, the courses also require thinking and conceptual skills, but at the college level these rarely (if ever) *replace* the "do" requirement. Therefore, procedural understanding is needed. Usually, students are required to know how to perform calculations by hand, even if calculators are allowed. Most college mathematics professors teach by lecturing, and that means students must take notes. Grades are determined for the most part by test scores. Test problems should not surprise students, as tests consist of similar problems to the ones students have worked. It is unlikely that a test would contain an essay question. It is equally unlikely that a college mathematics class would use class time on group discussions. Courses are certainly not integrated, and connections between courses are seldom made (except to perhaps refer to previously learned material). College mathematics courses are the opposite of NCTM-oriented curricula.

SOME REFORM IN COLLEGE MATHEMATICS

There are some small exceptions to the rule that college mathematics courses are traditional. I will not attempt to give a history of reform in college mathematics, but paint a picture of the current status. The reader should note that some current reform efforts are actually a return to previous reform efforts that were not successful.

One exception to the lack of reform efforts has been in the area of calculus teaching. Calculus used to be the first college mathematics courses that students took if they were on track for a mathematics, science, or engineering major. Now, some students are taking calculus in high school and starting at a later sequence in college. Regardless, college mathematics professors still consider calculus an appropriate beginning college course. Mathematics majors start with calculus and continue to take many more mathematics courses. Many other majors require a year in calculus, and then a student is finished with mathematics. All of this makes calculus a very important course.

Reform has been attempted in calculus. In fact, some mathematics professors will discuss calculus reform and will ask colleagues from other colleges if they teach reform or traditional calculus. Reform calculus has many of the characteristics of NCTM-oriented curricula. Reform calculus usually involves heavy use of graphing calculators and/or computers. Traditional calculus has many procedures (taking derivatives and integrals). Thus, much of traditional calculus is spent on learning how to do these procedures. Keep in mind, however, that when procedures are taught at the college level, the "why" (as in why the procedures work) is also taught, and students are required to understand the "whys." In reform calculus, the calculators do the procedures, so that the "why" is taught but not necessarily the "how." This frees up some time, and the remaining time is spent on building further conceptual understanding as well as problem-solving. Traditional calculus also spends time on conceptual understanding, but probably not as much time on problem-solving as reform calculus does. This is true because time is limited. In sum, the main difference between traditional and reform calculus is in how much time is spent on procedures, with more time spent on procedures in the traditional course.

Reform calculus also has an emphasis on group work. In fact, the problem-solving just mentioned is usually done in groups, as lab assignments. These labs consist of real-life situations that require calculus principles. Students work in groups, using technology (either calculators or computers), and give solutions to the problem. (Most of these problems have more than one solution.) Some type of results write-up (with English words, not just mathematics) is required.

Another component of reform calculus is the presence of multiple representations. Reform calculus professors often claim they teach according to the "rule of four." This means that for each problem, the students will look at four forms: symbolic, graph, table, and verbal.

Traditional calculus emphasizes symbolic manipulations and spends a little time on graphs.

Besides the components already mentioned, there is a writing emphasis in reform calculus courses. Instead of regular exercises, students are required to explain processes in writing. Exam questions may resemble essay questions. There is also an emphasis on discovery learning. Students will explore topics instead of listening to lectures. In general, in reform calculus, the emphasis switches from "how to do calculus" to "when to apply calculus and what it all means." Rather than "take this derivative" (reform calculus supporters argue that a calculator can do that), the question will be "Why would a derivative be the procedure in this situation?" A student might be expected to answer something like this: "Because a derivative is a rate of change, and that is what the problem needs." It is possible that the student would not be expected to find the actual derivative unless a calculator is used.

There has been considerable debate about reform calculus, and reform calculus is not the norm. Overall, mathematics professors like it when students can "do." Of course, they also like it when students know what to do without being told and when students know why they are doing what they are doing. But, mathematics professors tend to love mathematics, and they see the actual doing of mathematics as working the procedures.

Reform has popped up in other classes as well. In statistics, technology has replaced certain processes (for example, calculators have replaced the use of complicated tables that used to be in the back of the textbook) and certain procedures (for example, the use of computers has replaced time-consuming computations done by hand). Lab assignments are often used, as real-life data is easy to find in the area of statistics. Group work has replaced some of the lectures. But, there is no reform statistics as there is reform calculus. In other words, reform statistics has taken a moderate approach and not created debate.

Reform is occurring in courses below calculus. There are new courses intended for liberal arts majors. Some nonscience majors require a course in mathematics. In the past the course has been precalculus. It is now the attitude among many mathematics professors that it is silly to require precalculus and not calculus. After all, what purpose does the "pre" serve? So, courses have been developed that survey mathematics instead of preparing the students for a course that they are never going to take.

These liberal arts courses have components similar to those found in reform calculus (for example, the technology use and group work). It is significant that mathematics professors would allow courses out of the calculus sequence, and so the popularity of these courses is an element of reform as well.

College algebra is currently undergoing reform. College algebra is a course before precalculus and should be the responsibility of high schools. However, most colleges have placement tests to place incoming students into their first mathematics course. Since these placement tests consist mostly of algebra problems, many students are placed into an algebra course. So, colleges offer what should probably be called high school algebra, but since it is college, the course is called college algebra. College algebra is commonly taught in a traditional manner. However, there have been some reform efforts to make college algebra similar to NCTM's vision of algebra. Reform college algebra uses graphing calculators and is lighter on symbol manipulation. Reform college algebra is heavier on multiple representations and solving problems other than symbolically.

There have also been efforts to teach courses (including college algebra) online. Many of these efforts are to increase the student population. There is a national shortage of secondary mathematics teachers. Some of the online efforts are to retrain adults who have obtained bachelor degrees with a nonmathematics major. Since it is difficult for adults to leave their jobs and change locations, online mathematics courses offer a method of getting these adults back to college without the travel inconveniences and hardships. Mathematics, as you might suspect, is not an easy subject to teach online. I predict that we will see increased efforts in online mathematics teaching in the future.

MAJORING IN MATHEMATICS EDUCATION

As the reader can tell, the extent of reform in college mathematics is small. Even in the mathematics education of future teachers, NCTM standards have not had a significant influence. Students who major in mathematics education do not always major in mathematics as well. At some colleges, students do get a bachelor's degree in mathematics and also in teaching mathematics. Other colleges require only the teaching mathematics part. No one requires the mathematics part only, because in order to teach in a public K–12 school, teachers must be licensed. Licensing requirements include having taken many education courses.

In the teaching mathematics major, the student does take many education courses. Some of these courses are called "methods." It is in methods courses that students learn how to teach mathematics. The methods courses are taught by a mathematics educator. The mathematics educator will be in support of NCTM, and students will learn about the NCTM standards. Other education courses taken by future mathematics teachers will also be taken by future teachers of other subjects, as the courses are more general in nature and not specific to mathematics.

Teaching mathematics majors also take mathematics courses. These courses are taught in the mathematics department by mathematics professors. These courses usually do not contain any reference to NCTM. These courses are taught in the same manner whether the students are teaching mathematics majors, engineering majors, or any other major. This actually creates a disconnect for the future teacher, since most mathematics courses are more similar to traditional high school mathematics than to NCTM-oriented mathematics. Future teachers are *told* how to teach NCTM-oriented mathematics in their methods courses, but they do not learn mathematics that way in their mathematics courses. Teachers are not taught in the manner that they are taught to teach! One principle of NCTM is that students do not learn by being told something. Yet, they are told how to teach mathematics, and they do not learn mathematics in that context. They are told how to teach mathematics in a consistent manner with NCTM, but their actual mathematics courses are not consistent with NCTM.[1]

THE GAP

This disconnect between how mathematics teachers are taught to teach and how they are taught mathematics is not the only disconnect that occurs in the field of mathematics education. The disconnect between NCTM-oriented high school curricula and college-level traditional mathematics is a large concern. Mathematics education continues past high school for almost every student who attends any type of postsecondary school. Almost every major requires some mathematics.

In the case of the transition to college mathematics, "gap" might be a better word than "disconnect." There is a gap between high school mathematics and college mathematics. For the most part, students are expected to jump this gap without aid of a bridge. This gap has grown larger since NCTM-oriented curricula have arrived. Although the word "gap" is an easier word to envision than "disconnect," gap sometimes leaves the wrong impression. Gap seems to imply that mathematics curricula follow a straight line, that high school curricula leave students short on that line, and that college mathematics curricula begin farther down the line. This isn't quite right.

Mathematics curricula do not follow a straight line. It is not so much that high school curricula leave students behind as they leave students in a spot that does not connect with college curricula. And so there is this disconnect. In order to examine this closer, let us discuss where high school curricula leave students and where college curricula would like to pick them up.

When discussing high school students, we need to separate students who had traditional curricula from students who had NCTM-oriented. Let us start with the good news regarding the NCTM-oriented students.

Students from NCTM-oriented curricula generally leave high school with good problem-solving and communication skills. They can think mathematically in most situations. They can solve word problems. They can talk about what they are doing. They are quite good at using technology, especially calculators. They know a fair amount about traditional high school mathematics content. They know quite a bit about discrete mathematics, and probability and statistics, which are not usual high school mathematics content. They know a lot about functions and families of functions. For example, they can discuss exponential function behavior. (This is not a likely skill of traditional students.) They have a good conceptual understanding of multiple representations (graphs, tables, and equations).

But, there is a downside. The NCTM-oriented students know some algebra, but are not adept at solving algebraic equations. They do not have much memorized. They probably do not know the trigonometric identities. They are not good at performing algorithms or procedures. They probably do not know how to work with logarithmic functions by hand.

To discuss students from traditional curricula, we should probably just switch the two preceding paragraphs. In other words, what NCTM-oriented students do not do well, traditional students do. But, also, what NCTM-oriented students do well, traditional students do not. Students from traditional curricula are good at solving algebraic equations by hand. They are good at algorithms and procedures. They probably know how to work with logarithmic functions by hand.

Traditional students probably are not good at communicating mathematics. They know very little (if anything) about discrete mathematics, probability, and statistics. They are not adept at moving among representations (graph, tables, and equations) and probably do not even fully realize that there are different representations. They are not adept at using technology.

Now, here is the rub. Undergraduate mathematics professors expect incoming students to be good at algebra, to be able to work procedures, and to have a set of mathematical theorems memorized. And they expect that these things are true without the benefit of a calculator. That is it. It is not that college mathematics professors do not care about the rest, but that they do not need the rest to be in place yet. If the incoming student has what college mathematics professors expect, then anything missing can be handled at the college level. However, without what the college mathematics professors expect, the students will not be successful at college mathematics. In sum, college mathematics professors expect incoming students to have been successful at traditional K–12 mathematics. It is not true that college professors expect "better" students than they are getting, but that they expect traditional students. The NCTM-oriented curricula are not worse than traditional curricula, but they are different. And, college mathematics professors expect the traditional background.

We could bridge the gap, then, by going back to traditional mathematics curricula. Of course, this is precisely what traditional mathematics supporters want to do. The NCTM-oriented supporters certainly do not want to go back to traditional mathematics, and they offer four reasons why we should not.

First, we could bridge the gap by convincing mathematics professors that they are wrong in what they expect and want. If mathematics professors changed their expectations, that would also bridge the gap. If undergraduate mathematics education became more reform (as has been attempted with reform calculus), then the gap would be bridged. In other words, simply pleasing mathematics professors may not be in students' best interest. By the way, writers of NCTM-oriented curricula have personally told me that when they sat down to write their curricula, they were expecting that undergraduate mathematics education would change as well. At the time, calculus reform looked like it would catch on. But undergraduate mathematics did not change like it appeared that it would.

Second, other college courses (such as science and engineering) do want the algebra skills but could probably settle for a subset of the algebra skills. In addition, these other college courses can take advantage of NCTM-oriented students' superior problem-solving skills. Traditional mathematics will help college freshmen with mathematics courses, but NCTM-oriented curricula might be better for everything else, even science courses.

Third, even the traditional students do not have the level of algebraic (and other) skills that mathematics professors would like. In addition, NCTM-oriented supporters argue that traditional methods drove students out of mathematics with its "drill and kill" approach to learning. Returning to traditional might bridge the gap, but there would be fewer students to cross the bridge.

Fourth, there are compromise approaches that would not cause NCTM-oriented curricula or mathematics professors to change what they want. There are many ideas for these compromises. High schools and/or colleges could offer summer classes for students who have completed their senior year of high school before their freshman year of college. During this summer class, students would drill on the procedures, algebra skills, and identities that college professors want. Mathematics educators argue that research shows that when students learn the concepts first, it takes much less time to learn the procedures. Such a summer class might be very successful.

Another idea is to shut down the NCTM-oriented curricula halfway through high school students' senior year. The last semester can be as I described in the preceding paragraph. Or, NCTM-oriented curricula could supplement their materials with units for the college-bound that do what I am describing. These extra units could drill on algebraic techniques and things of that nature. In fact, there are currently some high school NCTM-oriented curricula that have National Science Foundation funds to create these supplementary units.

Whether you accept one of these four objections or want K–12 schools to return to traditional mathematics, one thing is certain. As it stands, the NCTM-oriented curricula leave students at a spot that mathematics professors do not expect. And thus these students are left with a disconnect, a gap, in their learning, which makes their transition from high school mathematics to college mathematics a difficult one.

I want to end this chapter by telling you about a survey I conducted in my home state of Minnesota.[2] I asked one member of the mathematics department at every four-year college and a representative sample of community colleges in Minnesota the following question: What do you see as the three main differences between learning mathematics at the high school level and learning mathematics at the college level? I was amazed that almost everyone gave the same three answers. Here they are.

First, they said that students must learn how to read a mathematics textbook when they get to college. In high school, students are more inclined to turn immediately to the problems or possibly look for an example in the textbook to help with the problems. However, students might not actually read the textbook. In college, not all material is presented, and the student must read the textbook.

Second, they said that students in college are responsible for their own learning. This might mean literally to learn on their own, or with other students, or even to make good use of the professor's office hours. But the initiative rests with the student. Even attending class is a decision of the individual student. Although some professors might take attendance, this is not common.

The third thing they said was that the pace is quicker and the depth of coverage deeper at college than in high schools. This is not a value judgment against high schools. It is simply format. Rather than a 170-some-day instructional year in high school, students might meet 55 minutes for 39 classes in college. The same material needs to be covered, and probably the college course has more emphasis on proofs.

Neither NCTM-oriented nor traditional curricula will better prepare students on these three essential points. I think it is true that a good student with good study habits will do well in college no matter what high school curriculum she had or what college mathematics professors expect. Of course, as a nation, we need to be concerned about all students, and not just the really good students. Yet it is reassuring that good students are good students, regardless.

SUMMARY

There is no equivalent to NCTM-oriented curricula at the college level. Reform has affected college mathematics education, but not to a significant degree. Calculus reform has been attempted, but has not become a popular method for teaching college calculus. When curriculum directors were developing high school curricula, they believed that reform, such as calculus reform, would be successful at the college level. This has not materialized.

There does exist a gap from high school mathematics to college mathematics, because high school mathematics is aligned with NCTM standards and college mathematics is not. Various ideas could help bridge the gap.

Besides the gap from high school to college, future mathematics teachers also experience a disconnect. Future high school teachers are not taught mathematics in the same manner that they are told to teach mathematics.

CHAPTER 10

What Is Happening Internationally in Mathematics Education?

Although the citizens of the United States like to think of the nation as the best in the world, that is far from true in regard to mathematics education. International testing occurs on a regular basis. The best known and current set of studies goes by the acronym TIMSS, which stands for Third International Mathematics and Science Study. With more than forty countries, five grade levels, and over half a million students, TIMSS examines students, teachers, and principals. Results given here are as current as the year 2000. Examining the eighth-grade students in the United States puts the United States in a tied position with thirteen other countries. Unfortunately, the tied spot has twenty countries scoring significantly higher than the United States, and only seven countries scoring significantly below. Of course, an interesting question is what are those twenty countries doing that we are not. To answer this question, we will briefly examine mathematics education in Japan as well as compare the mathematics knowledge of Chinese elementary teachers to American elementary teachers.

JAPAN

Japan does a much better job providing mathematics education to students than the United States. However, if we are going to learn from the

Japanese, we will have to change many things, including some things that may be very difficult to change. It will not be enough to change our curricula.

Japan has approximately half the population of the United States while being confined to a geographic area about the size of Montana. Even within that, approximately 80 percent of the land is mountainous. Japanese life is uniform. They are of one race, one language, one diet, one custom, and one education. They are fiercely loyal to each other and to any group to whom they belong.

Japanese people believe in *gambae*. *Gambae* means that one is successful if one works hard enough to be successful. One's attitude and behavior must match this belief that hard work leads to success. In the United States, many students and parents believe in innate mathematics ability; that is, one is successful in mathematics if he was born to be successful in mathematics.

Japanese parents believe that the education of their children matters more than anything. Within the home, parents set up special places equipped with desks for their children to use while studying. This is not a small feat when one realizes how small most Japanese homes are.

Japanese students believe that their job is to learn. If a student makes a mistake, he is not unhappy, but glad to find an area for improvement. Mistakes are a good way to learn. In the United States, mistakes are to be avoided. This Japanese view of mistakes allows the teacher to send to the blackboard any student who has a wrong answer. The student can then share his thinking process. By examining incorrect processes, the entire class gains a deeper understanding of the correct process. In the United States it is considered mean to single out a student who has made a mistake. But much less can be learned from praising a student who did a problem correctly than from examining incorrect work.

Class size is actually much larger in Japan than in the United States. Class size in Japan is a minimum of forty students. Also, the Japanese school year is longer than the United States school year. The United States school year is roughly 175 days and Japan runs school for 240 days. Each school day is longer in Japan as well. In addition, Japanese students are never removed from the classroom for some other activity (such as an assembly, a music event, or a sports event). Lessons are never interrupted with notes from the office or an announcement over the intercom. These types of distractions are absolutely unacceptable in Japan.

Mathematics education is very important in the overall Japanese curriculum. At first it seems surprising that Japanese children have less homework than American children. However, this is a bit deceiving. There is a private tutoring system in Japan called *juku*. *Juku* is held after school, and students drill on mathematics facts and procedures (among other things). While it is true that Japanese students have less homework, the *juku* takes its place. Japanese students work very hard in the evenings and/or on the weekends with *juku*.

Japan has a national mathematics curriculum that everyone follows. There is a strong emphasis on mental arithmetic (doing arithmetic without the aid of pencil-and-paper and certainly without a calculator). This emphasis far surpasses the emphasis that either traditional or NCTM-oriented curricula place on mental arithmetic in the United States. Calculators are not a part of the Japanese curriculum. Still, their mathematics problems are complicated and challenging.

The pedagogy follows a set process. The teacher introduces a problem, which has more than one solution. Students work together in small groups on the problem. Exploring, conjecturing, pattern-finding are all normal activities within the small groups. At the end of class, the teacher leads the entire class in a discussion about the results. Sometimes different groups of students will present their solution process to the entire class. Finally, students are assigned two to four problems to use for practice. (Japanese problems are similar to problems in NCTM-oriented curricula, and not to problems in traditional curricula.)

Each time this process is followed (teacher poses problem, students investigate problem, teacher leads the wrap-up), it is called a lesson. These lessons are viewed as extremely important. Their construction is far from haphazard. Each lesson is formed through an eight-step process. First, the teacher defines what it is she wants the students to learn. The teacher will then look through books and journals to come up with ideas on what type of problem or activity would get the students to learn what has been defined. Third, the teacher tries out the lesson in a class while other teachers watch. Then the teachers meet and talk about the lesson. The teacher revises the lesson based on their input. The revised lesson is taught, with the group of teachers watching again. The seventh step is another group meeting, with evaluation provided. Finally, the teacher revises the lesson one more time and then makes the lesson available for all the other Japanese teachers in the nation.

These lessons are not part of the students' textbooks, but are available to every teacher.

Another important component of Japanese mathematics education is how the teacher is treated. There are far more teachers than positions for teachers. (The United States has a national shortage of mathematics teachers.) Teaching is a good job in Japan. Teachers are treated like professionals. Besides the original education that teachers receive, ongoing extensive in-service is required. This in-service includes attending programs (at least twenty days a year), and at least one to five days of specifically updating content and pedagogical knowledge. Also, some teachers are labeled master teachers. Non–master teachers spend two days a year watching the master teachers teach. Japanese teachers are so thoroughly trained that despite the national curriculum, textbooks are very thin. In other words, Japanese teachers have learned the national curriculum. Teachers create lessons and, in a sense, that is part of the national curriculum, but the lessons are not part of the textbooks. Japanese teachers do not, in any sense of the word, teach by a textbook as do American teachers. Japanese teachers are given much more preparation time during the school day than American teachers. By Japanese legislation, all public teachers and college professors have the highest rank and salary in Japan.

James Stigler has conducted numerous research studies comparing Japanese and American mathematics education.[1] He concludes that there are three main differences. Japanese teachers center their lessons on students' thinking. Japanese teachers facilitate students' thinking by setting up lessons that will encourage students' thinking. Students' thinking is very important to Japanese teachers. As you can tell, all three differences center on students' thinking. Japanese teachers build specific times into the lessons for students to think. Outside of class, Japanese teachers predict what students will be thinking and form responses to various thought paths. Japanese teachers design questions that will bring out students' thinking, no matter which path the students are taking.

Some NCTM-oriented supporters have argued that Japanese lessons are similar to NCTM-oriented lessons. And they are. Besides the similar pedagogy, Japanese mathematics curriculum is integrated and includes probability and statistics content. In fact, Japanese teachers more often display NCTM-oriented behavior than American teachers do.

However, it is not fair to conclude that the United States should use NCTM-oriented curricula if we want to be like Japan. There are two reasons. First, significant parts of the Japanese curriculum are not at all like NCTM-oriented curricula. The boldest example of this is the complete opposite view on calculator use. The second reason is the *juku* system mentioned before.

The *juku* system is made up of private (and profit-making) schools run separately and independently of the regular schools. *Juku* is affordable and available to most people. The percentage of students who attend *juku* is around 40 percent in grade five and rises to about 50 percent for grade seven. By the ninth grade, close to 70 percent of all ninth graders attend *juku*. If the regular day is like NCTM-oriented curricula, *juku* is like traditional mathematics. And so, Japanese students get both!

We cannot use Japan as a model to settle our math wars unless we use Japan as a reason to find a balance of both traditional and NCTM-oriented. Also, before deciding to go with what Japan does, we should look at the other countries that are ahead of the United States in international testing. One is Germany. The majority of emphasis in German mathematics education is on developing procedures. This would be an argument for traditional mathematics. I do not want to give all the background of German mathematics education that I would need to give in order to defend or refute this argument. The point is, there is no *one* method for teaching and learning mathematics that has been successful. *Many* methods have been successful. But, even if we do not make a math wars conclusion, there is a lesson we can learn from Japan, and apply to mathematics education in the United States.

If we want to learn from Japan, we should look at the roles that individuals play in the entire mathematics education system. Parents are actively involved in their children's mathematics education. Parents consider education, and mathematics education in particular, as the most important family project that they undertake. Despite cramped housing, study areas are set aside for children, and desks and supplies are provided. Parents make their high expectations clear to their children.

Children in turn take responsibility for their learning. They believe that ability is not innate but comes from hard work. During school and *juku*, children take an active involvement. They do not blame the teacher when they fail to understand something. They pursue until they are able to understand.

Teachers in Japan are among the most respected professionals in the nation. Teachers take this rank seriously. They work hard to get degrees in teaching and continue to improve their teaching each year. They view their job as a true profession that requires continual training.

The roles that parents, students, and teachers fulfill in Japan are at a much higher level than the roles we give parents, students, and teachers in the United States. I believe it is nothing short of this type of dedication on everyone's part that will allow the United States to do as well as Japan. It would be nice if we could change curricula, which has always been the attempt in the past. It will take so much more.

The United States does not treat our teachers as professionals. Treating teachers as professionals will call for enormous change, and, unfortunately, will not be an easy fix. Certainly raising teachers' salaries would help, but that in itself is not enough. One thing we need to do is raise the standards of schooling. We need to take the best students in mathematics majors and train them as teachers. As it stands, the best mathematics majors are often discouraged from becoming teachers. It is courageous to make it harder to become a mathematics teacher and thus at least temporarily reduce the number of mathematics teachers, because we are in a time of national shortage of mathematics teachers. Yes, while we already do not have enough mathematics teachers, we should allow fewer of them to be mathematics teachers. However, raising the quality of mathematics teachers is more important than increasing their quantity, and, eventually, increased quality will lead to increased quantity, too. Other equally difficult changes will have to be made. The needed changes are analogous to the changes needed to lose weight. Weight loss will be permanent only with a considerable change in eating and exercising habits. Nothing short of that will work. However, most people would prefer not to commit to that degree. Most people would prefer to try a new diet fad and not make permanent attitude and lifestyle changes. We cannot just try new mathematics curricula. We need an attitude, and, yes, a lifestyle change.

Another idea, if we really want to commit to NCTM-oriented teaching, is to have mathematics teachers teach half days. The remaining part of the day will be devoted to retraining teachers how to teach in an NCTM-oriented fashion, including training in both pedagogy and mathematics content. Of course, reducing the amount of time teachers spend teaching would be very expensive.

CHINA

Shifting focus, let us examine an aspect of mathematics education in China to see what lesson we might learn from the Chinese. In 1999, Liping Ma published a study based on her dissertation. Ma's study has been applauded by both mathematics professors and mathematics educators. It is rare that both sides of the math wars agree that a study is significant. For that reason alone, I would like to describe it.[2]

Ma began her career as an elementary teacher in China. She eventually earned a master's degree and then decided to move to the United States to pursue a doctorate in mathematics education. She did earn a Ph.D. in mathematics education by working with both Michigan State University and Stanford University.

Ma's study compares the mathematical knowledge of elementary teachers in China to elementary teachers in the United States. The bottom line of the study is that Chinese teachers know more. What matters about the study is how Ma went about making the comparison.

The first thing Ma did was describe a concept that she labeled PUFM, which people pronounce puff-im. The label of course is an acronym and stands for profound understanding of fundamental mathematics. Ma was not just interested in teachers' understanding of elementary mathematics. She wanted to know how deep the understanding was.

Ma's motivation for her study was that Chinese students significantly outperform American students on international mathematics tests. As we have done with Japan, educators try to find differences between Chinese and American curricula and pedagogy. Ma suggested that Chinese elementary teachers know more mathematics than American teachers. This suggestion seemed preposterous because American elementary teachers study much more mathematics than Chinese elementary teachers. Ma persisted with her belief that Chinese elementary teachers know more mathematics even though they are less educated mathematically than American teachers. This led her to examine closely the type of mathematics knowledge that elementary teachers have. Is it possible that while American teachers have more mathematical knowledge, Chinese teachers have deeper mathematical knowledge?

In trying to clear up this question, Ma defined PUFM; that is, profound understanding of fundamental mathematics. Fundamental could be replaced with the word elementary. Fundamental means the mathematics taught in K–6 grades. Fundamental also means foundational. Truly, K–6 grade mathematics forms the foundation upon which all of higher mathematics rests. Future mathematics study is dependent on understanding K–6 mathematics. Fundamental also means primary. By primary, Ma means that K–6 mathematics contains the beginnings of higher mathematics. Pattern-building is the beginning of algebra. Examining properties of shapes is the beginning of geometry.

But what does Ma mean by profound understanding? If one has profound understanding of a mathematical concept (in this case from the elementary curricula), he can perform the associated procedure and is aware of the conceptual structure behind the concept. Ma says that one needs a breadth, depth, and thoroughness to one's understanding to have PUFM.

Breadth is reflected in understanding how the concept is connected to other mathematical concepts. Depth comes in being able to look at the concept from multiple perspectives; to be able to represent the concept through various means (pictures, graphs, verbal descriptions, mathematical equations, and tables are some examples). Depth might be represented as one's ability to offer more than one explanation to a student who is trying to learn the concept. Depth is also represented through the ability to identify the main mathematical subconcepts. In any particular mathematical concept, there are subconcepts. There are probably two or three subconcepts that are key and make the overall concept work. A depth of understanding is shown when one can identify the key subconcepts within a mathematical concept. A good teacher will point these out and put special emphasis on these for students.

Thoroughness is demonstrated by one's ability to understand the mathematics that surrounds the mathematics that one is using. A second-grade teacher shows thoroughness when she understands how recognizing a pattern is really the beginning of algebraic thought. If that teacher also recognizes how pattern recognition fits into algebra and understands the bigger piece of algebra itself, then the teacher is showing thoroughness.

Ma gives a nice analogy. How do you know the city streets in the city in which you live? If you just moved to the city, you probably know a limited number of routes (perhaps from home to work, home to a grocery store, etc.). If you have lived in the city longer, you may know how to get to many places. You may know how to get from home to the movie theater. However, it is possible that you know only one route to each place and have not explored additional routes. If you have lived in the city a long time, you know many routes, and with the help of a map could probably find any location. But, consider a taxi driver in the city. The taxi driver knows how to get everywhere, and probably by many different ways. Maybe during rush hour a certain route is better than another route. The taxi driver knows where the speed traps are. The taxi driver can find places even without an address. The taxi driver has a profound understanding of fundamental "traverse the city." A teacher with PUFM is like the taxi driver who has a profound understanding of the city streets.

Ma hypothesized that American teachers do not have PUFM, and that Chinese teachers do have PUFM. American teachers have more mathematics knowledge in some sense. They have taken more mathematics courses and can do more procedures. But Chinese teachers have deeper mathematics knowledge. They fully understand what they are doing. To test her hypothesis, Ma devised methods for testing both procedural knowledge and PUFM. The procedural knowledge was easy to test. She simply gave teachers mathematics problems that required procedures to find the solutions. PUFM was more difficult to test. Ma had several ideas on how to test PUFM.

She decided that one way was to ask the teachers to put a given procedure into a word problem. In other words, ask teachers a strictly computational (procedural) elementary mathematics problem, such as division of two numbers. After the teacher solves it, then ask the teacher to make up a word problem so that the solution will require the student to work the same procedure (the same division) that the teacher just worked. Ma hypothesized that being able to go beyond the procedure to create the word problem would show PUFM. Another method for measuring PUFM was to ask the teacher to explain the why behind the procedure; that is, why is the procedure what it is.

The results were that American teachers could work most of the procedures but did not do well on the PUFM parts of the test. Chinese teachers did well on both procedures and PUFM.

One situation involved subtraction and asked the teachers to explain why the subtraction procedure works. All of the teachers (American and Chinese) could perform the subtraction. But only 17 percent of American elementary teachers knew, while 86 percent of Chinese teachers knew why the subtraction procedure works.

Another situation involved multiplication. The teachers were shown a multiplication problem (123 times 645) and asked to give the answer. Also, the teachers were shown an incorrect algorithm that a student had performed and asked the teachers to describe what they would say to the student. Every teacher could perform the multiplication. Only 39 percent of the American teachers could offer an explanation of why the incorrect algorithm was mathematically incorrect, while 92 percent of the Chinese teachers could do so.

Another situation required the teachers to perform a calculation with fractions and then create a word problem that represented the computation. This time many American teachers could not do the procedure. In fact, only 43 percent of American teachers could perform the computation, while 100 percent of the Chinese teachers could. None of the American teachers could create a correct word problem to represent the operation. All of the Chinese teachers could.

Ma investigated further ideas and problems, but the results are even more dismal for the United States, so let us stop where we are. The Chinese teachers had PUFM while the American teachers did not. Ma took the study further in trying to determine how the Chinese teachers developed PUFM. Ma concludes that Chinese teachers formed the foundation for PUFM in their own schooling, but fully developed PUFM as they taught. Ma concludes that if the United States wants to improve mathematics education, we will have to improve the mathematics knowledge of our teachers.

Improving the mathematics knowledge of teachers should occur in three stages. We need to improve the mathematics education of our teachers when they are K–12 grade students. We need to improve our college-level teacher training. Finally, we need to improve our teacher support, or our in-service program, so that PUFM can develop as the teacher teaches.

Ma also suggests that the United States should fix the disconnect between how teachers learn mathematics and how they learn how to teach mathematics. This is the disconnect mentioned in chapter 9. We teach teachers to teach according to NCTM standards, but that is not how they learn mathematics.

Ma concludes her book with a moving plea for balance. It is in her last few pages that she endears the love of both mathematicians and mathematics educators. For Ma says clearly, it is important not to throw out the old for the new. Although never using these words, she pleads for balance between traditional and NCTM-oriented. If the United States is to learn from China, then we should find the balance between the two sides. Ma says, "My study indicates that teachers with PUFM never ignore the role of 'procedural learning' no matter how much they emphasize 'conceptual understanding'."[3] By procedural, she is referring to traditional mathematics, and she uses conceptual to refer to NCTM-oriented mathematics. Of course, NCTM-oriented people will argue that they do not ignore the procedural. Traditional supporters argue that NCTM-oriented curricula *do* ignore the procedural. It works the other way, too. The NCTM-oriented people argue that traditional ignores the conceptual. Traditional supporters say that they do not ignore the conceptual. But, we have already discussed this business of having your cake and eating it, too. Both sides are guilty of that thinking.

In our "touch of international" chapter, we have recognized that most countries score better than the United States on international testing in mathematics. We have looked at Japan's mathematics curriculum and at the mathematics knowledge of Chinese elementary teachers. From Japan we can begin to understand the level of fundamental (in fact, may I say profoundly fundamental) change that needs to be made in the role of students, teachers, and parents. From China, we can begin to understand the changes that need to be made in the education of teachers, beginning in kindergarten. For our purposes, though, there is a conclusion that both the Japan and China data support. We need to find a balance. Japan has both traditional and NCTM-oriented curricula by combining their school day and *juku*. China teaches their teachers to have both kinds of mathematics knowledge. Ma pleads for the procedural and the conceptual. And truly, it makes little sense to know how to do (traditional) but not why (NCTM-oriented). But, it also makes little sense to know why (NCTM-oriented) and not how (traditional).

SUMMARY

Students in the United States have performed poorly on international standardized testing compared to students in other nations. Japan mathematics curriculum is similar to NCTM-oriented curricula. However, Japan also has *juku* school, which is similar to traditional curricula. In addition, the entire nation of Japan is very supportive of education.

A recent study has shown that teachers in the United States and teachers in China seem to understand how to perform procedures equally well. However, teachers in China have a much deeper understanding of mathematics; that is, they have profound fundamental understanding of mathematics.

CHAPTER 11

Both Sides of the Question

The goal of this book is to provide you with the necessary tools to take an informed position on the math wars. The goal of this chapter is to summarize both sides of the math wars, so that near the end of the book are concise statements about the issues. This level of compactness would have been too difficult to understand at the beginning of the book. In chapter 1, I set the scene with the following paragraph.

> The National Council of Teachers of Mathematics (NCTM) has written and disseminated two sets of standards (the second is a revision of the first). Most mathematics educators (people who do research in mathematics education) believe that NCTM is correct with their standards. Most current mathematics curricula are written to support the standards; I will call them NCTM-oriented. Quite a few (but not all) mathematicians and parents, and other stakeholders, believe that NCTM is mistaken about several issues; they think that the NCTM-oriented curriculum is not a good approach and they want mathematics education to return to the more traditional curriculum. Thus, the math wars debate: those in favor of NCTM and those against.

We can now handle that paragraph without the simplifications. The easiest simplification to fix is that NCTM published two additional volumes as part of the standards (one on teaching and one on assessment). These two volumes have not caused the disagreements that the two curriculum volumes have.

The larger simplification concerns the dichotomous manner that I used in presenting the case. The issues are not so black and white as to have only two sides. The math wars are heated, and there are many people on each side who think it is impossible to compromise. Nevertheless, many people not only think it is possible to compromise, but believe it is important to reach a compromise. In this sense, the math wars have three sides: NCTM-oriented, traditional, and those who want a balance. But even this is not the whole picture. As stated in chapter 5, there are numerous players in the math wars who do not really have a side or who bounce back and forth between sides.

The history of mathematics education reveals a lack of compromise. Throughout the history of schools, mathematics education has swung from one set of beliefs (and the corresponding curriculum and pedagogy) to an opposite set of beliefs. The stage was set for the math wars in the 1980s. During that decade the National Council of Teachers of Mathematics (NCTM) came into power. The NCTM was formed in 1920 but did not have a strong influence on mathematics education, even though having an influence was their goal, until the 1980s.

Various factors allowed NCTM to come into power. The history of the pendulum swing from one end to another built an atmosphere of unrest and created a desperate search for answers. The fact that American K–12 students were scoring dismally on international mathematics standardized tests helped create a climate for acceptance of NCTM. After all, the situation was bad, and NCTM said they could fix it. Why not let them try?

The NCTM published three sets of standards. The most important was the 1989 set of curriculum standards. This set of three was revised and combined in 2000, to bring the complete set of standards to a total of four volumes. The standards call for a radically different mathematics curriculum and pedagogy. The National Science Foundation was convinced that NCTM was correct and offered grants to curriculum developers who were given the task of writing a curriculum that honored the NCTM standards. The resulting curricula are the so-called NCTM-oriented curricula.

Parents' and mathematicians' reaction to NCTM-oriented curricula (their disapproval of it) started the math wars. The math wars is the term used to describe the heated debates between the NCTM-oriented camp and those against NCTM. As mentioned, one manner in which I simplified the paragraph was to disregard people who are neither completely for nor completely against NCTM standards. Many, many people accept and like aspects of the NCTM standards and disregard and dislike other aspects. Most mathematics educators support NCTM. Those who do support NCTM support the NCTM standards nearly 100 percent. The other side of the math wars includes mathematicians. However, it is not true to say that most mathematicians are actively anti-NCTM. Most mathematicians have never heard of NCTM. And again, some very informed people want a balance between NCTM-oriented and traditional.

In fact, another simplification was in stating that those against NCTM want to return to traditional. They actually do not want to return to traditional per se. They want to return to traditional but include some improvements. Most people on the traditional side of the math wars acknowledge that traditional was not working very well. However, they do not think that NCTM has the answer. The answer lies in better education of our teachers both in content and pedagogy. The traditional side wants a better (an improved) traditional. They do not want to return to bad traditional. In a sense then, the traditional side is calling for a type of balance that tips more toward traditional than toward NCTM.

So, as one can see, this balance idea is in itself a difficult goal to achieve. Some supporters of NCTM have argued vehemently that opponents of NCTM use polarization to attempt a return to traditional curricula. However, here is the problem. Write a curriculum by starting with a NCTM-oriented curriculum and adding some traditional, and call this Curriculum A. Write another curriculum by starting with a traditional curriculum and adding some NCTM-oriented, and call this Curriculum B. If we now had the same results, that is, if Curriculum A and Curriculum B were very similar, the math wars could be resolved. But, the result is different depending on which curriculum you start with and which curriculum you add. The problem with this "start with one and add in some of the other" is that the curriculum takes on the philosophy of the "starting" curriculum. The additional curriculum acts like a supplement. In this manner, there is not a true balance.

Supplements are fine. In fact, it is probably true that NCTM-oriented with supplemental traditional would be acceptable to most people, even most people involved in the math wars. Only the strongest opponents of NCTM-oriented would be unhappy with NCTM-oriented and supplemental traditional. And, NCTM-oriented supporters are working in the direction of supplementary traditional. That is why they do not like arguments that emphasize the polar views. Those arguments make it harder for critics of NCTM to be satisfied.

Some supporters of traditional, however, will not be satisfied with NCTM-oriented and supplemental traditional. Here is why. Those who are the strongest supporters of traditional mathematics curricula treat mathematics as a special, beautiful discipline, much like music. And like the study of music, they are not concerned that mathematics applies to everyday life. Being involved in mathematics (doing mathematics) is like making beautiful music; we do it because it makes humanity stronger and more noble. We educate our children in mathematics to make them better people.

Traditional supporters will argue that if we "water down" mathematics curricula to NCTM-oriented, we have lost this view of mathematics. We have changed mathematics to something similar to music appreciation. Students in music appreciation can no longer perform classical music, but they have an appreciation for music and for those who can perform. To perform classical music, one learns notes, practices scales, and memorizes musical pieces. There are a lot of procedures and much rote memorization and drill in music. The most radical traditional supporters argue that students need the pieces that will allow them to perform mathematics someday, not just appreciate it. Although not all students will go on to be mathematicians, that is the nature of K–12 education. Not all students go on to be any particular thing, but this nation believes in a level of general education for everyone on significant subjects (science, mathematics, English, and social studies).

It is because of this basic philosophy of why we educate, and in particular why we have students study mathematics, that some traditional supporters cannot accept NCTM-oriented with supplemental traditional. By the way, traditional with supplemental NCTM-oriented would pretty much be traditional. Traditional has always included some NCTM-oriented. Of course, one could increase the amount of NCTM-oriented material. But, the point is, finding the balance is not a straightforward process.

In sum, traditional with supplemental NCTM-oriented is likely to be unacceptable to those who are NCTM-oriented, but NCTM-oriented with supplemental traditional will be acceptable to most people on both sides of the math wars. However, the last option will not be acceptable to everyone on the traditional side. Either way, a *balance* will not be reached by mixing one with some of the other. It will take much more creativity than that.

Let us turn now to summarizing both sides of the math wars. I will begin with the NCTM-oriented side. For the ease of reading, I am going to set this section aside and talk as a supporter of NCTM-oriented mathematics. I want to do this so that I do not have to precede my sentences with "according to NCTM supporters." I will then do the same for the traditional side.

THE NCTM-ORIENTED SIDE

Mathematics education is not working. At best, traditional mathematics educates the college-bound. In reality, traditional mathematics educates a subset of the college-bound who go on to be mathematics majors. Other students do not need the advanced algebraic techniques, practice with proof, and many other topics in the traditional sequence. Traditional mathematics does not prepare students for the workplace, either. Employers want employees who can think—the other problem with traditional mathematics. Traditional mathematics consists of out-of-date content, it lacks use of modern tools (calculators), and the pedagogy is not reflective of what we now know about learning (for example, knowledge cannot be transmitted). The NCTM-oriented curricula include the basics, but it is time to define the basics as they ought to be defined in modern terms.

Traditional mathematics has an emphasis on procedures with a near exclusion of concepts. In other words, students do not learn the "whys" behind the procedures. Although procedures are a part of mathematics, they are a small part. Traditional mathematics also spends too much time on basic computational skills. The skill-and-drill approach is killing off interest in mathematics. In sum, traditional mathematics relies on drilling (without understanding), memorizing (without understanding), and working word problems according to memorized algorithms (without understanding). By the way, students do not tend to remember memorized mathematics anyway. It is difficult to remember what we do not understand.

The alternative is to alter radically the curriculum and pedagogy. Students need conceptual understanding. They need to understand why they do what they do. This is more important than having them learn the specific procedures, because calculators can perform those procedures. Other content, such as discrete mathematics, probability, and statistics should be brought into the curricula as well. The world has changed. We need mathematics that is applicable to this world.

In addition, students should have mathematical experience with open-ended problems—the types that actually occur in everyday life and in the workplace. Students who have studied under traditional curricula have no ability to deal with open-ended problems because they have never had practice with them.

Also, to fit the modern world, students should use calculators. Calculators are powerful tools not only for doing mathematics, but for building an understanding of mathematics. Calculators are available and a part of life. Calculators will not go away. It is time to incorporate them fully into mathematics curricula. Concepts that can be replaced by a calculator should be replaced by a calculator. Calculators are not replacing arithmetic skills. Students are learning these skills at the same time. Even if calculators do replace arithmetic skills, those skills are not as important as the other things that students are learning with the aid of technology.

Processes like communication, representation, problem-solving, reasoning, and connections are more important than any particular content. It is important to give students an overall feel for mathematics, including numbers. This does not occur with traditional curricula. Communication is an important component of NCTM-oriented curricula. If students cannot communicate mathematically, what good is their mathematics knowledge? Communication is virtually ignored in traditional curricula. Rather than presenting mathematics in fragments, NCTM-oriented curricula give a holistic view of mathematics.

The pedagogy needs to change as well. Students should grapple with their own mathematical thinking. Teachers should not be tellers of information. Students must construct their own understanding. Telling things to students does not result in learning. Telling things to students at best results in parrot math; that is, the students might be able to parrot back to the teacher what they have been told.[1]

Students do not learn in isolation. Workplaces are not set up with individuals working alone. Students need experience solving mathematical problems in groups. Groups of students are able to construct mathematics.

The NCTM-oriented curricula are not just someone's best ideas. Extensive research has shown that NCTM-oriented curricula are successful. Students do as well as traditional students on standardized tests, on college placement tests, and in college. If NCTM-oriented students are a little behind traditional students in areas like algebra manipulation or computational skills, they quickly catch up. Learning the conceptual first makes the procedural easier to learn. By the way, research also has shown that traditional mathematics does not work.

Future teachers do not need more mathematics courses. Future teachers need courses that teach them how to teach mathematics. Let's start educating our teachers in the modern methods.

Returning to traditional curricula replays history. History has shown that when a new mathematics education movement is beginning to work, the pendulum swings. Give NCTM-oriented curricula a chance to establish itself.

In summary, NCTM-oriented curricula include content that traditional curricula do not, and a change of focus from memorization and drill to thinking and problem-solving. NCTM-oriented teaching is done to build connections and involve all students actively. All children should be constructing their own mathematics. NCTM-oriented mathematics allows all students (not just the college-bound) to actively build problem-solving ability with the aid of today's tools. Calculators can replace tedious calculations. Important mathematics is mathematics that makes sense to students, and that is necessary in today's world. NCTM-oriented curricula consist of today's mathematics and will result in a mathematically literate adult population. This is the goal of K–12 education, not to build unnecessary skills.

THE TRADITIONAL SIDE

NCTM-oriented curricula are a disaster. They ignore basic computational skills, procedures, and paper-and-pencil by-hand symbol manipulation (the heart of algebra). Students from NCTM-oriented curricula will need to take remedial mathematics courses at college, because they will not place into the first college mathematics course. Students from NCTM-oriented curricula will have to add extra years of college time if their major is mathematics or science. Students leaving high school will fall in a gap that NCTM-oriented curricula have created between high school and college mathematics. The colleges are not equipped to bridge the gap for students short on traditional content. The extra content (discrete mathematics, probability, and statistics) that NCTM-oriented students have learned is not needed. There is only so much time for K–12 schooling, and the basics are most important.

Although procedures are not all of mathematics, procedures are a very important part of mathematics. Reform movements in mathematics should call for better teaching of procedures, not for procedures to be removed from curricula. If teachers knew more mathematics, they would teach procedures in such a manner that they would make sense to students.

The basic skills that are being omitted in NCTM-oriented curricula form the foundation of mathematics. The NCTM-oriented curricula build their concepts without a base. Concepts built in air will not stand. Calculators are replacing thought processes that students require. Long division, for example, explains the base number system. Students should learn this for themselves and not depend on calculators. Concepts that calculators replace are fundamental to mathematics and to a future understanding of higher mathematics.

Some concepts in mathematics do have to be memorized. People memorize certain facts and procedures in all areas of life. The world would not run smoothly if people were not willing to memorize anything. There is nothing inherently bad about memorizing.

Another mistake that NCTM-oriented curricula make is in giving "fuzzy" definitions. Mathematics is a precise science. Definitions must be detailed. NCTM-oriented curricula try too hard to decrease the distance between school mathematics and everyday mathematics. In so doing, the science of mathematics is lost. Mathematics is not supposed to be so imprecise as to be an everyday occurrence. The everyday nature of mathematics can be found in arithmetic, in algebraic thought, and in logical thinking. However, there is much more to studying mathematics. In addition, it is not necessary to set every problem in a real-life setting, which makes it difficult to teach the required mathematics. It is better to teach mathematics, and then show a few applications.

Research that supports NCTM-oriented curricula was conducted by the curriculum directors. Research that expresses concern with NCTM-oriented curricula does not get published. Journals are either run by

NCTM or are NCTM sympathetic. Research has been published in other countries that support traditional mathematics. Further, research has always supported the current fad. New Math is an example.

Teachers do not understand how to teach according to NCTM-oriented principles. Teachers do not learn mathematics in an NCTM-oriented manner. It takes training that is not being provided to learn how to implement NCTM-oriented curricula. This training should start with kindergarten teachers and move up as students progress. Having a mixture of NCTM-oriented curricula with traditional is the worst possible situation for students.

Traditional mathematics contains the mathematics that mathematicians believe is necessary. If we want an educated society, then students need to be educated mathematically. Mathematics educators do not have enough understanding of mathematics to make curriculum decisions. If traditional mathematics is not working, then the answer is to improve teacher quality by improving the mathematics ability and knowledge of teachers. More mathematics should be required to obtain teaching licenses. It is true that considerable problems exist with traditional education. These problems can be corrected by better teaching, not by changing the curriculum.

In summary, traditional mathematics is the mathematician's mathematics. It contains procedures, memorization, drill, concepts, problem-solving, algebraic manipulation, word problems, arithmetic, geometry, proofs, reasoning, and thinking. Traditional mathematics gives the foundation of mathematics to the college-bound and to the not college-bound. The purpose of K–12 education is to provide the foundations of all disciplines, including mathematics. A few students will go on to be mathematicians, but it is not necessary that everyone become a mathematician. Traditional mathematics curricula are not perfect and have not been taught perfectly (teacher preparation needs to be improved). But let us not throw out the baby with the bathwater.

CALL FOR BALANCE

I cannot resist ending this chapter with a call for balance. As other nations have done (for example, Japan and China), we need to have both aspects of mathematics in our curricula. This balance must go beyond settling on one side and then supplementing with some of the other. That is not a true balance.

The reader has enough information now to make up his or her own mind. Unless we do as Japan does (with school during the day and *juku* at night and/or on weekends), we cannot take all of traditional and all of NCTM-oriented mathematics and put them together. Perhaps you want

Table 11.1
Main Differences Between NCTM-Oriented and Traditional Mathematics

NCTM-Oriented	Traditional
Mathematics as needed for applications	Mathematics for mathematics' sake
Nonroutine problem-solving	Routine problem-solving
Conceptual	Procedural
Extensive use of technology	Light use of technology
Students will learn basic facts as they learn mathematics	Drill in order to learn basic facts
Has support of mathematics educators	Has support of mathematicians
Uses technology to solve algebra problems	By-hand solution of algebra problems
Statistics, probability, discrete mathematics	Light on statistics, probability, and discrete mathematics
Less aligned with standardized testing, college placement tests, and college mathematics	More aligned with standardized testing, college placement tests, and college mathematics
Heavy on mathematical processes such as communication, representation, problem-solving, and connections	Light to no presence of mathematical processes
Light on computations	Heavy on computations
Use of calculators to handle real-life data	Absence of real-life data
Development funded by NSF	No major funding
Constructivism	Platonism
Emphasis on why	Emphasis on how
Research backing	Little faith in research
Open-ended problems	Traditional word problems
No tracking	Tracking
Mathematics for all	Mathematics especially for the college-bound
Up-to-date approach	Old-school approach
Critical nickname: "Fuzzy math"	Critical nickname: "Parrot math"
Group work, discovery learning, teacher as facilitator	Lecturing, practice exercises, teacher as teller
Mathematical modeling	Absence of mathematical modeling
Strength: Students learn to think mathematically	Strength: Lays a foundation of algorithmic thinking needed for higher mathematics
Weakness: Fails to teach the basic skills, including arithmetic and algebra	Weakness: Students learn to do, but they do not understand why

to advocate for one side or the other. Or perhaps you want to advocate for a balance. If so, you must think through how this balance could actually be achieved. People who do not support NCTM are often accused of creating dichotomies, but no one on either side has suggested an acceptable balance in order to eliminate the dichotomies. Table 11.1 provides, at a glance, the main differences between NCTM-oriented and traditional mathematics.

CHAPTER 12

Additional Resources

This completes our short course in the math wars. Because you may want further information, and because mathematics education will continue to change, I want you to be aware of resources. The best sources are websites, published materials, and networking.

It is dangerous to put web page addresses into print form, because they are subject to change. Yet web pages are often the best sources of information because they are so current. I will compromise by listing essential web pages only.

The National Council of Teachers of Mathematics (NCTM) maintains a website at http://www.nctm.org. You will find a summary copy of the NCTM standards among the up-to-date information regarding NCTM.

Some of the mathematicians on the mathematicians' side of the math wars also maintain a website. It is called the Mathematically Correct site and can be found at http://mathematicallycorrect.com. There you will find position statements for the traditional side.

The final two websites give information about international and national testing. The TIMSS (Third International Mathematics and Science Study) data can be found at http://timss.bc.edu. The National Center for Educational Statistics also provides mathematics test data at http://nces.ed.gov/.

Of course, you can use Google, or any other search engine, to find mathematics education websites. In particular, all of the NCTM-oriented curricula maintain project websites. Search on the name of the curriculum, and you should find an address. If you are aware of authors who write about mathematics education, you can also search using their names to find their latest publications.

Besides websites, this author believes in the power of books to convey information about mathematics education! Printed copies of the NCTM standards can be obtained by ordering them directly from NCTM. NCTM's website will allow you to shop, or you can write NCTM at NCTM Headquarters Office, 1906 Association Drive, Reston, VA 20191-1502. Throughout this book, the notes provide reference information for all the books and articles referenced. I want to make special mention of three.

Ma's book that was referenced in chapter 10 is quite easy to read. Her book is called *Knowing and Teaching Elementary Mathematics* and is published by Lawrence Erlbaum Associates.

The book I mentioned in chapter 4 (*Standards-Based School Mathematics Curricula: What Are They? What Do Students Learn?*) is a good book for reading about the research that supports NCTM-oriented curricula. It is also published by Lawrence Erlbaum Associates.

James Stigler has coauthored two books that are easy to read and contain a lot of mathematics education information. I recommend both *The Teaching Gap* (James W. Stigler and James Hiebert) and *The Learning Gap* (Harold W. Stevenson and James W. Stigler). Both are published by Simon & Schuster. I used these books while writing chapter 10.

Journals are another source of information. Currently most of the published journals support the NCTM-oriented side, and so you might want to balance reading them with reading other sources. The NCTM publishes three journals that are of a practical nature. The reader can locate information about them at the NCTM website. These journals are aimed at teachers, not parents. Some general education journals run special theme issues on mathematics education. I have always found *Phi Delta Kappan*, for example, to be sensitive to mathematics education issues and to be more balanced than NCTM publications. I also like *American Educator*.

If you want further information or future resources, you may want to become actively involved in shaping mathematics education. This will most likely require involvement with others. You could return to school to take courses in mathematics education. Perhaps more realistic for busy lives would be to attend conferences and meetings about mathematics education. The NCTM holds many local, state, regional, and national meetings. The Mathematics Association of American does as well, although these are not specifically to address mathematics education, but to address mathematics. Still, some of the speakers will talk about the teaching and learning of mathematics. Meetings of your local school district, including Parent Teacher Association meetings, will certainly address mathematics education, at least from time to time.

The NCTM has a chapter in each state as well. For example, in my state it is the MCTM, the Minnesota Council of Teachers of Mathematics. At the state level you will find many people with interest in mathematics education who are willing to talk about the issues. Many state-level organizations publish newsletters, which are a good source of information as well.

You can call your local colleges and schools in order to speak to people interested in mathematics education. At the K–12 level, this includes secondary mathematics teachers, and possibly a mathematics specialist or curriculum director. If you find people who have a personal and professional interest in mathematics education, you will increase your sources of information. You can ask, at the school district level, to see copies of the mathematics textbooks that are used. This might be your best chance at seeing NCTM-oriented curricula up close. If you have children in elementary school, you might volunteer to help during the mathematics class. You might learn a lot yourself!

Websites, books, journals, active involvement through conferences, and networking are all sources of information regarding mathematics education. The math wars, and mathematics education in general, needs the involvement of teachers, parents, scientists, mathematicians, students, politicians, and businesspeople. Mathematics educators are important, but they do not see the situation from every perspective. I believe that the only way to end the math wars and come to a balance between NCTM-oriented and traditional mathematics is to have the active involvement of many people.

Appendices: More Details on Related Issues

This series of appendices presents more information on issues related to mathematics education but only touched upon in the chapters of this book. Although not as central to the math wars as the other issues covered in more detail in the chapters of the book, the three related issues are gender differences in mathematics ability, definitions of mathematics, and placement testing.

Appendix 1:
Gender Differences in
Mathematics Ability

Gender differences in mathematics ability refer to the long-held belief in society that girls are not as good in mathematics as boys. When schooling began, it was predominately intended for men, and, actually, only for men of high social standing. It was not expected or accepted that women would even take mathematics courses, let alone do well in them. This thought process changed slowly. Consider this quote:

> In the 1870s, a physiologist at Harvard, Dr. Edward H. Clarke, admitted that young women could learn rigorous subjects but argued that they should not. In particular Clarke opposed the admission of women to Harvard.... A young woman might learn algebra, but [he argued] when the limited sum of energy flowed to the overwrought brain, it harmed the natural growth of ovaries.[1]

Clearly, women were not to be studying mathematics. Besides the possibility of harming her ovaries, many parents believed that if their daughters were to be good in mathematics, they would never be married, as no man would want to marry a woman who does mathematics.

Today these points of view are humorous. And yet, there remain beliefs in society that females do not do as well in mathematics as males.

This belief transfers to very real peer pressure placed on girls in middle and high school to "dumb down"; that is, appear to be less able in mathematics than one actually is. The punishment for being too able in mathematics is lack of running with the in-crowd and lack of having a boyfriend. Parents need to help their daughters have enough sense of self that they achieve at their true ability level.

But is this ability level the same for girls as it is for boys in the area of mathematics? Mathematics education research has shown small differences in mathematics ability in favor of boys. Before pursuing this further, it is important to qualify the term "small." In fact, all students, regardless of gender, range quite widely in mathematics ability. Although in experimental studies there is often a significant statistical difference between boys' and girls' mathematics performance, the term "significant" does not mean large. It is used in a statistical sense to mean that the small difference found was probably not due to random fluctuation, or chance. When one says that a study was significant at the .05 level, for example, it means that there was about a 5 percent chance (or less) that the data were obtained by chance (and there actually is no difference). Thus, the differences between girls and boys in mathematics performance are real. But they are very, very small. In fact, if one takes the difference between the mathematics ability of two randomly selected boys, it is as likely to be larger than the difference between a randomly selected boy and a randomly selected girl than it is likely to be smaller or the same. One researcher summed it up this way: "Consistent between-gender differences are dwarfed by much larger within-group differences."[2] If you are the parent of sons and daughters, there is no more likelihood that the sons are better in mathematics than the daughters than that one son is better in mathematics than another son.

Putting the differences in perspective then would actually allow one to dismiss that there are large issues in terms of gender differences in mathematics performance. Still, there are small differences, and it is interesting to wonder as to their cause. Research has shown that the cause is not biological; that is, there is nothing about being female that causes one to do less well in mathematics than males. However, researchers do believe that there are sociological differences involved.

In short, society expects higher mathematics performance from boys than from girls. Schools treat boys differently from girls. Mathematics teachers often treat girls differently from boys. As mentioned, peer groups treat boys differently from girls. It is more socially acceptable for a boy to be good in mathematics than for a girl. (And, actually, it is more socially acceptable for both boys and girls to do poorly in mathematics than to do well.) Even the toys that society tends to give to little boys are more conducive to promoting mathematics skills than the toys that girls tend to receive. Parents also have been guilty of treating their sons differently than their daughters, including passing on gender attitudes about mathematics.

Wider society has an influence as well. Although publications now make an effort to be nonsexist, in the past, mathematics textbooks were full of word problems with males doing mathematical things. Girls, if they showed up as characters in word problems at all, were sewing or cooking. Mathematics textbooks aside, culture, even today's culture, has a negative portrayal of those who do mathematics. This portrayal is still predominately of males doing mathematics, not females.

Societal pressures also lead to related issues that influence mathematics learning. For example, girls are not taught to persist, as are boys. Mathematics ability takes a great deal of persistence. Girls are not taught to have internal confidence, which is also an asset in mathematics learning. Girls are also taught to fear success, and that, too, does not go along well with mathematics learning.

It is possible, for a variety of reasons, that the NCTM-oriented curricula have the ability to reduce the small gender differences. For example, the NCTM-oriented curricula are heavy on communication, and society views girls as more gifted in communication skills than are boys. Because of the variety of learning opportunities under NCTM-oriented curricula, the curricula are more likely to appeal to more people, including girls. The shift in curricular focus under NCTM-oriented curricula may also ease societal pressures that favor males. Since NCTM-oriented curricula are so new to parents, there may not be the expectation that boys will do better than girls. In a similar manner, teachers may have no preconceived ideas about boys and girls under NCTM-oriented curricula. In short, because of the nature of the curricula and the newness of them, NCTM-oriented curricula may turn out to appeal to girls more than traditional curricula do.

Regardless, it is important that parents are aware that the common perception that girls are not as good in mathematics as are boys does not have a lot of basis in truth. It is true that there do exist small differences between girls and boys in mathematics performance. These differences are even smaller when viewed next to the large differences in mathematics ability in general between any two people. Finally, society is to "blame" for these differences, and parents need to play a role in ending the differences.

Appendix 2: Definitions of Mathematics

I teach undergraduate mathematics courses. One of my students once wrote this on an essay that he submitted: "It is important to recognize that as one's study of mathematics deepens, the definition is subject to change." This is true. Yet most people, including parents, believe that mathematics is an unchanging body of facts and procedures, and that is how traditional mathematics curricula present mathematics. The NCTM-oriented curricula tend to present mathematics as a dynamic science, quite capable of change.

Although it is actually not true that mathematics is unchanging, it can be argued that K–12 mathematics ought to be presented that way. In numerous disciplines, the "truth" must be simplified as a new learner is introduced to the discipline. Of course, it can also be argued that the truth need not be simplified to that degree.

Since this discussion about the nature of mathematics is rather theoretical and short on practical applications, it has only been touched upon in this book. However, it is an interesting theory to explore. It is true that different curricula have different results, one of which is to change students' views of mathematics.

To illustrate this, I will give some quotes from my students. At the beginning of an advanced undergraduate mathematics course, I asked my students to define mathematics. These students are all currently high school mathematics teachers. Here is a sampling of responses that I received.

- Mathematics is a science that uses rational reasoning to come to a conclusion that is deemed logical by the system and rules set by the science.
- Math is a way to study and understand the world.
- Mathematics is the use of numbers and variables to figure out why things are the way they are and also to figure out how we can achieve other things.
- The main use of mathematics is to solve problems and make things clear.
- Mathematics is an intimidating, complex way of thinking.
- Mathematics is the study of numbers.
- Mathematics is a system of rules and symbols used to define the universe and how it works.
- Mathematics is the tool we use to help understand and describe things around us.

At the end of the semester, I asked this same group of students to tell me what mathematics is. Especially interesting to me is the fact that every student changed his or her answer. Here are some responses at the end of the semester.

- Math is huge.
- Mathematics is the source of order in life.
- Mathematics is what enables humans to make sense of creation.
- Mathematics is a very valuable game.
- Mathematics is a realm of thinking that we have created.
- Mathematics is a thought process.
- Mathematics is a very important addictive game.
- The average person probably would say that mathematics is arithmetic, algebra, numbers, or something along that line. It is hard to describe this word that we all love and see as beautiful. Mathematics has a certain beauty to it, but the average person cannot see that beauty because you have to have a deep understanding and love of mathematics in order to see it. This beauty is what makes mathematics hard to describe. My definition has changed. And if I were asked again I am sure it would change again.

As students progressed in their study of mathematics, their definitions became broader. Students' definitions move away from a view of mathematics as a product and toward mathematics as a process. This movement occurs naturally as students study advanced mathematics at the undergraduate level. This phenomenon is unlikely to occur for K–12 grade students. However, NCTM-oriented curricula are more likely than traditional curricula to facilitate this movement.

Appendix 3:
Placement Testing

Every undergraduate mathematics department has some process for placing students into their first mathematics course, even if that process is simply to trust the students to sign up for the courses that they think are correct. However, the vast, vast majority (research has estimated 99 percent) of mathematics departments have a placement system in which the department plays a rather significant role, which usually includes, but is often not limited to, giving a test. Many departments require that incoming freshmen take a mathematics test during orientation, and the results of the test inform the students of which mathematics course to take first. If a test is the only piece of the placement system, it tends to not work very well.

Placement tests tend to be highly algebraic in nature. They are written by mathematicians, who tend to be traditional. Students from NCTM-oriented curricula do not perform as well as those from traditional curricula on placement tests. Some NCTM-oriented curricula are in the process of being supplemented with special units for the college-bound, which will prepare a student for placement testing. As it stands, if a student has not reviewed by-hand symbol manipulation, the student will be placed into a college algebra course. However, research, including my own, has shown that these placements are probably incorrect.[1]

Many, many things go wrong with placement testing, some of which would not be all that difficult to fix. For example, placement tests are often given in the summer during orientation. Students quickly forget much of what they have learned once summer hits. However, a quick review would bring it back into students' working minds. Unfortunately, this quick review does not occur, and students end up taking a complete course that they may not need to take. In addition, placement tests are often given first thing when students arrive (so that there is time to have the results ready for students before they leave orientation). Students, many of whom have gotten up early in the morning to travel to the college, are suddenly hit with a mathematics test. Mathematics anxiety will bloom under such conditions.

Even if all the conditions are made perfect and students review the material before taking the placement test, a placement test does not tend to be successful in its placement abilities. Undergraduate mathematics courses are difficult for most students. This is not due just to the disconnect in content in the NCTM-oriented high school curricula and undergraduate mathematics courses, but because of the differences in college versus high school in general. In college, students must be responsible for their own learning. Students might have to study mathematics for the first time. It is often the case in high school that if a student attends class and works at the mathematics during class, she does not have to work at studying the mathematics on her own. Making the adjustment from high school to college often takes considerable time. A placement test cannot predict how well a student will make that adjustment.

In addition, there are adjustments that must be made that have nothing to do with either mathematics or study skills. Most students are living away from their parents' home for the first time. This adjustment takes energy, time, and emotions that in turn take away from students' ability to do well in courses. Again, a placement test will not predict how well this will go for students.

Besides all of these factors that placement tests do not take into consideration, there is also difficulty in determining exactly what they do or should measure. Placement tests are not designed to determine all the mathematics that a student knows. Rather, they are designed to measure a subset of the mathematics skills that a student possesses. The tested subset is determined by mathematics professors, based on what they think is needed to be successful in various college mathematics courses. Thus, it is not a measure of what was learned in high school. In addition, many mathematics educators do not agree that what is on placement tests really will prove to be needed in mathematics courses. Mathematics professors tend to be of the belief that students must enter Calculus I (normally the first mathematics course a student will take in college) with strong algebra skills. Thus, placement tests are filled with algebra manipulations. Although most college calculus courses are taught in such a manner that algebra is needed, it is still possible that students can recall or even learn the algebra as they go. In addition, there is debate about whether college calculus courses ought to be so algebra-dependent.

Using a test as the only measure of placement is not a successful method. It would be better to have a *placement system* that considers other factors, with the test being one factor. Other factors could include the courses taken and grades received in high school, how well the student did overall as a high school student, the level of confidence that a student has in doing mathematics, and the scores a student received on high school standardized tests in mathematics. Whether the student was in NCTM-oriented or traditional mathematics in high school should also be considered.

Truly, a student needs individual advising in order to determine what class to take first in college. This type of advising is sometimes provided by mathematics professors if the college is small enough. Even if a college professor does advise a student, it would be best if the student also sought the advice of a high school mathematics teacher. Their high school mathematics teachers will have a very good idea what course each student is prepared to take in college.

Placement testing is a difficult issue for most colleges, because placing students correctly is a very difficult task. As parents, it would be wise to have your child find out what the placement system is at the college he has chosen. Encourage your child to ask his high school mathematics teacher where she thinks the student ought to start in college mathematics. (If the student is ultimately placed much differently from the high school teacher's suggestion, the student should ask to speak with an adviser at the college.) Second, find out from the teacher if she knows good methods for preparing for the placement test. It is possible that the college has a practice placement test online. Students should practice by taking that online test and sharing the results with their high school mathematics teacher. Ultimately, the problem with placement testing and the placement system is, it is an attempt by colleges to reach into the high schools and help smooth the transition. It would be much better if somehow the high schools and colleges could each meet the student halfway.

Two final comments are important. First, research has suggested that how successful a student is in a first college mathematics course has little to do with anything except one factor: whether or not the student took mathematics in the senior year of high school. Taking mathematics (any mathematics) during the senior year of high school greatly increases the probability that the student will be successful in college mathematics. Second, it is true that placement tests are traditional in nature, and thus students in NCTM-oriented curricula must practice and/or learn algebra skills prior to taking placement tests.

Glossary

An Agenda for Action: Report written by the National Council of Teachers of Mathematics in 1989, which promoted the idea that problem-solving ought to be the center of mathematics curricula. It set the stage for the first standards document.

Assessment Standards for School Mathematics: Book written by the National Council of Teachers of Mathematics (NCTM) in 1995, which put forth a set of standards about testing. It is one of four standards documents published by NCTM.

Back To the Basics: Period from 1975 to 1979 in which mathematics curricula consisted of arithmetic operations and other routine procedures.

Basic skills: Skills that are considered basic in mathematics involve memorizing or executing simple procedures. Examples include addition, subtraction, multiplication, and division of real numbers (including whole numbers, integers, fractions, and decimals). Simple procedures include working with percents, finding the price per unit, and unit conversions.

By-hand symbol manipulation: Process of solving algebraic equations without the aid of technology.

CAS: Computer algebra systems, found in most graphing calculators, allow the calculators to solve algebra problems symbolically.

Cognitive science theories: Class of theories about mathematics learning which claims that a student receives mathematical knowledge from a teacher (or another student) and reconstructs that knowledge for herself. The reconstruction might involve forming connections.

Constructivism: Theory of mathematics learning that claims it is impossible to transmit knowledge from teachers to students. Rather, students must actively construct their own knowledge. Pedagogy consistent with constructivism assigns the role of facilitator to the teacher.

Curriculum: Complete package of content, assessment, lessons, and pedagogy for a subject. Although a curriculum includes textbooks, it is not limited to textbooks.

Curriculum director: Person employed by a school district to make curriculum decisions. The curriculum director is not a teacher, but an administrator. Among other duties, the curriculum director selects curriculum, oversees standardized testing, and ensures that legislative requirements are met.

Curriculum and Evaluation Standards for School Mathematics: Book written by the National Council of Teachers of Mathematics (NCTM) in 1989, the first of an eventual four volumes. This volume initiated the math wars.

Discovery learning: Pedagogy in which students experiment in order to discover the rules. In the case of mathematics, theorems and procedures would not be told to students, but students would have to form conjectures based on evidence.

Elementary mathematics: Kindergarten through sixth-grade mathematics. Traditional elementary mathematics is heavy on basic skills.

Formalism: Theory of mathematics that describes mathematics as a very formal game. Under this theory, mathematics is similar to chess.

Fuzzy math: Derogatory term applied to NCTM-oriented curricula. Fuzzy means that the exactness of mathematics has been lost and any algorithm is acceptable.

Logicism: Theory of mathematics that describes mathematics as a system of logical rules.

Math anxiety: Fear of mathematics and studying mathematics.

Math wars: Heated debates between the NCTM-oriented and traditional side about mathematics curricula.

Mathematically correct: Group of mathematicians who are vehemently opposed to NCTM-oriented curricula.

Mathematician: One who holds an advanced degree (probably a Ph.D.) in mathematics and works in industry, government, or teaching.

Mathematics: Branch of science dealing with the practices of structure, logic, relations, numbers, measuring, quantifying, and shapes of objects. Numerous definitions for mathematics exist with little in common.

Mathematics education as a major: One who majors in mathematics education and studies both mathematics (although usually not in as much depth as needed) and education. A person holding a Ph.D. in mathematics education conducts research in the teaching and learning of mathematics.

Mathematics education: The formal teaching and learning of mathematics at any level (kindergarten through postgraduate).

Mathematics educator: One who holds an advanced degree (probably a Ph.D.) in mathematics education and works mostly in either a mathematics department or an education department (this is more likely) at a college or university. Some work for the government (such as for the National Science Foundation or a state education department).

Mathematics professor: One who holds an advanced degree (probably a Ph.D.) in mathematics and works at a college or university doing research, teaching, and professional service.

Mathematics specialist: A curriculum director assigned only to the subject of mathematics.

Mathematics standards: Usually refers to the National Council of Teachers of Mathematics set of standards or principles. Other organizations, such as state education departments, might also have mathematics standards, although they are usually aligned with the NCTM standards. Mathematics standards are as close to a national curriculum as the United States comes.

Mathematics teacher: One who teaches mathematics at the secondary level (roughly seventh through twelfth grades). (Most elementary teachers also teach some mathematics, but they call themselves elementary teachers, not mathematics teachers.)

Mile wide, inch deep: Mathematics curriculum that covers many subjects but with little depth. Mile wide, inch deep especially refers to a curriculum that spirals. Spiraling curriculum is integrated, with many different topics covered in one year. The idea is to teach each topic lightly, but then keep returning to it year after year (each year at a supposedly greater depth).

A Nation at Risk: Document published in 1983 by the Department of Education. It claimed that the United States system of mathematics education was failing.

NCTM: The National Council of Teachers of Mathematics is a powerful organization. The vast, vast majority of mathematics educators follow and believe in the precepts of the NCTM.

NCTM-oriented: Curricula (or philosophies) based on the standards and principles of the National Council of Teachers of Mathematics.

New Math: Period from 1950 to 1971 in which mathematics was taught in a formal manner. Symbolism and formalism were pushed beyond any K–12 grade students' ability to comprehend.

New New Math: Derogatory term applied to NCTM-oriented curricula. Although NCTM-oriented curricula have nothing to do with New Math, the term is used to imply that NCTM-oriented curricula are as much of a disaster as New Math was.

Nonroutine problem: Mathematics problem for which the students do not have a memorized procedure or algorithm to solve the problem.

Open-ended problem: Mathematics problem for which possible solutions are not given (that is, not multiple choice). Also used to mean a problem for which there are many different solutions, depending on what direction the problem is pursued.

Parrot math: Derogatory term applied to traditional mathematics. Represents students mimicking back to their teacher mathematics facts that students have memorized but do not understand.

Pedagogy: System, methods, and philosophy of teaching.

Platonism: Theory of mathematics that believes there is one and only one true mathematics.

Postsecondary mathematics: Mathematics taught at the college level.

Principles and Standards for School Mathematics: Book written by the National Council of Teachers of Mathematics (NCTM) in 2000, which both updated and consolidated the three previous standards volumes.

Problem-solving according to NCTM: Finding a solution path when the path is not obvious. True problem-solving requires problems to be nonroutine, and prefers problems to be open-ended.

Problem-solving according to traditional: Finding a solution path when the path is not given. Solving procedural problems are problem-solving, as long as the student is not told what procedure to use. Problems may be routine, and in fact a certain number of routine problems are necessary for learning problem-solving skills. Prefers that problems are not open-ended.

Problem-solving as an era: Period between 1979 and 1989 in which mathematics curricula was absent of basic skills and full of word problems.

Professional Standards for Teaching Mathematics: Book written by the National Council of Teachers of Mathematics (NCTM) in 1991, which put forth a set of standards about teachers. It is one of four standards documents published by NCTM.

Progressive education: Period between 1920 and 1950 in which the nature of the child was the most important educational factor. Discovery learning was the main pedagogy.

PUFM: Profound understanding of fundamental mathematics.

Qualitative: Research in which the data gathered is descriptive.

Quantitative: Research in which the data gathered is numeric.

Reform calculus: Undergraduate calculus presented by the "rule of four" (graphs, equations, tables, and descriptive). Nonreform undergraduate calculus is usually taught only as procedures, with equations. Reform calculus has a conceptual emphasis.

Reform mathematics: Same as NCTM-oriented mathematics.

Routine problem: Mathematics problem for which the solution path consists of a memorized procedure.

Secondary mathematics: Mathematics curricula for seventh through twelfth grades.

Sociological theories: Class of theories about mathematics learning that claims students cannot learn in isolation. Students learn by being apprentices in the company of masters (teachers). Students also learn by interacting with each other.

Standardized testing: Testing that is done under standard conditions, content, and scoring, with the purpose of being able to compare students.

Technology: In mathematics education, technology is calculators and computers.

Time of NCTM: Period beginning in 1989 and continuing through the present. Mathematics curricula is NCTM-oriented.

TIMSS: Third International Mathematics and Science Study, an international standardized testing study in which involved nations are ranked on mathematics and science teaching and learning.

Traditional: Curricula (or philosophies) that are *not* based on the standards and principles of the National Council of Teachers of Mathematics and might differ from those principles in substantial ways. For example, a traditional mathematics curriculum is much less calculator-dependent than an NCTM-oriented curriculum.

Notes

CHAPTER 1

1. See *One Field, Many Paths: U.S. Doctoral Programs in Mathematics Education*, edited by Robert E. Reyes and Jeremy Kilpatrick, and published by the American Mathematical Society in cooperation with the Mathematical Association of America in the year 2000.

CHAPTER 2

1. See "Doctorates in Mathematics Education: An Acute Shortage," in *Notices of the American Mathematics Society*, written by Robert E. Reyes, published in the November 2000 issue (vol. 46, no. 10, pp. 1267–1270).

2. This phrase (a mile wide and an inch deep) was actually invented long after the time of New Math and used to criticize traditional mathematics curricula. Later, it was applied retroactively to New Math. Ironically, it is never applied to NCTM-oriented curricula. However, NCTM-oriented curricula are often integrated (which means instead of separate yearlong mathematics courses, students study a little of everything each year). This integrated nature is similar to a mile wide and an inch deep. However, NCTM-oriented supporters will argue that the depth covered is thicker than an inch! The phrase then is used as a criticism of traditional mathematics, but may apply to various mathematics curricula.

3. I relied on a few sources while writing the New Math portion of this chapter. In particular, I used an article by David Klein entitled "A Brief History of American K–12 Mathematics Education in the Twentieth Century," published in *Mathematical Cognition* (edited by James Royer) by Information Age

Publishing in the year 2003. I also relied on an unpublished article entitled "Brief Chronology and Dramatis Personae of the New Math (1951–1975, R. I. P.)" written by Ralph A. Raimi and received by me through an e-mail listserve on January 12, 2004. In addition, Jeremy Kilpatrick wrote "Five Lessons from the New Math Era" and published it on a website, http://www.nas.edu/sputnik/kilpat2.htm, which I downloaded on January 23, 2004.

4. This quote is found on the first page of the book *Conquering Math Anxiety: A Self-Help Workbook*, written by Cynthia Arem, published by Brooks/Cole Publishing Company (Pacific Grove, California) in 1993.

5. *Math: Facing an American Phobia* is written by Marilyn Burns and published by Marilyn Burns Education Association in 1998.

6. *Agenda for Action* was published by the National Council of Teachers of Mathematics (and written by them as well) in 1980. The NCTM is headquartered in Reston, Virginia.

7. *A Nation at Risk* was written by the National Commission on Excellence in Education and published in Washington, D.C., by the U.S. Government Printing Office in 1983.

8. A copy of *A Nation at Risk* can be found at http://www.ed.gov/pubs/NatAtRisk/index.html.

9. Besides the references used for New Math, I also made use of the Thirty-second Yearbook of the National Council of Teachers of Mathematics (published by them in 1970) entitled *A History of Mathematics Education in the United States and Canada*.

CHAPTER 3

1. The movie *Good Will Hunting* was produced by L. Bender and directed by G. Van Sant and made available from Miramax, New York, in 1997. The *Mirror Has Two Faces* was produced and directed by B. Streisand and made available in 1996 by TriStar of Culver City, CA. *A Beautiful Mind* was produced and directed by R. Howard and made available in 2002 by Universal, Universal City, CA.

2. Janelle Wilson and I wrote an article on this topic: "Nerds? Or Nuts? Pop Culture Portrayals of Mathematicians," *et cetera*, 2001, vol. 58, pp. 172–178.

3. As with the history of mathematics education, I have relied heavily on sources for information about learning theories. In particular, I used *Theories of Mathematical Learning*, edited by Leslie Steffe, Pearla Nesher, Paul Cobb, Gerald Goldin, and Brian Greer, Lawrence Erlbaum Associates (Mahwah, NJ) in 1996. I also used *Philosophy of Mathematics Education* written by Paul Ernest and published by Falmer Press (Bristol, PA) in 1991. This is not to suggest that any of the authors/editors will agree with my own interpretations.

4. Here, too, I have relied on an outside source, *Philosophy of Mathematics*, edited by Paul Benacerraf and Hilary Putnam, published by Cambridge University Press in 1983.

CHAPTER 4

1. Larry Copes and I wrote an article published in 2003 called "Can We Reach Definitive Conclusions in Mathematics Education Research?" for *Phi Delta Kappan* (vol. 85, issue 3, pp. 207–211), which discusses the limitations of mathematics education research.

2. This study was published in 2003 in a journal called the *Mathematics Educator*. It was called "Testing the Problem-Solving Skills of Students in an NCTM-Oriented Curriculum" (vol. 13, issue 1, pp. 5–14).

3. My coauthor (Kay Wohlhuter) and I had this study published in 2004 in *FOCUS: On Learning Problems in Mathematics* (vol. 26, no. 1, pp. 23–33). The article is called "Beginning Secondary Mathematics Teachers: A Snapshot across One State."

4. The *Handbook of Research on Mathematics Teaching and Learning* was published by Macmillan Library Reference (Simon & Schuster Macmillan, New York) in 1992. The editor is Douglas Grouws.

5. *Standards-Based School Mathematics Curricula* was published by Lawrence Erlbaum Associates (Mahwah, NJ) in 2003. Sharon Senk and Denisse Thompson are the editors.

6. This quote is on page 120 of an article by Hal L. Schoen and Chris. R. Hirsch published in 2003, called "Responding To Calls for Change in High School Mathematics: Implications for Collegiate Mathematics." It was published in *American Mathematical Monthly* (vol. 110, pp. 109–123).

CHAPTER 5

1. This study was part of my Ph.D. dissertation, *Assessing NCTM Standards-Oriented and Traditional Students' Problem-Solving Ability Using Multiple-Choice and Open-Ended Questions*, completed in 2000 at the University of Iowa.

2. The book is called *California Dreaming: Reforming Mathematics Education*, written by Suzanne Wilson and published by Yale University Press (New Haven and London) in 2003.

3. This quote can be found on the website for the California Department of Education, http://www.cde.ca.gov/.

4. This quote and further information can be found on the website for the New York Department of Education, http://www.nysed.gov/.

CHAPTER 6

1. The four standards documents are all published by NCTM, out of Reston, VA.

2. This is on page 1 of the 1989 document.

3. The term "decreased attention" is used for the first time on page 21 of the 1989 document, and then used throughout the document while describing each of the standards.

4. This can be found on page 21 of the 1989 document.

5. This can be found on page 71 of the 1989 document.

6. This can be found on page 96 of the 1989 document.

7. This can be found on page 144 of the 2000 document.

8. This quote was taken from a publication of NCTM's entitled *Answers To Frequently Asked Questions about Principles and Standards for School Mathematics.* This publication can be found on the NCTM's website (http://www.nctm.org).

9. This can be found on page 25 of the 2000 document.

CHAPTER 7

1. *Math Trailblazers* is published by Kendall/Hunt, and a website can be found at http://www.math.uic.edu/IMSE/MTB/mtb.html.

2. *Connected Mathematics* is published by Prentice Hall, and a website can be found at http://www.mth.msu.edu/cmp/.

3. *Contemporary Mathematics in Context* is published by Glencoe/McGraw-Hill, and a website can be found at http://www.wmich.edu/cpmp/.

4. This quote was taken from a chapter, "High School Mathematics Curriculum Reform: Rationale, Research, and Recent Developments," in a book, *Annual Review of Research for School Leaders* (editors are P. S. Hlebowitsh and W. G. Wraga), published in 1998 by Macmillan Publishing Company of New York (pp. 141–191; the quote is on p. 153). H. L. Schoen and S. W. Ziebarth wrote the chapter.

CHAPTER 8

1. This item was taken from the Core Plus curriculum (Course 3, page 208), published by Glencoe/McGraw-Hill.

CHAPTER 9

1. Another problem that occurs with the education of future teachers is that many teachers (especially at the elementary and middle school level) are

licensed to teach mathematics at grade levels that are actually beyond their ability to understand. Very little mathematics is required of elementary teachers, for example, and elementary teachers are sometimes licensed to teach up to grade eight. Algebra is often a grade eight course. However, these problems with major requirements are beyond the scope of this book. Certainly changes must be made, but these changes are not an issue of the math wars per se.

2. This particular set of results can be found in a column that I author. At the time this book was being written, I wrote a column in the bimonthly newsletter of the Minnesota Council of Teachers of Mathematics (MCTM). This column reports on survey results from questioning mathematics professors across the state of Minnesota. The column discussed here and other columns can be found at MCTM's website: http://www.mctm.org/.

CHAPTER 10

1. I have relied on James Stigler's work in writing this section on Japanese mathematics education. Stigler's books are very readable. I would recommend *The Learning Gap* (by H. W. Stevenson and J. W. Stigler, published by Simon & Schuster, New York, 1992), and *The Teaching Gap* (by J. W. Stigler and J. Hiebert, published by Simon & Schuster, New York, 1999).

2. Liping Ma's book is entitled *Knowing and Teaching Elementary Mathematics*. It was published in 1999 by Lawrence Erlbaum Associates (Mahwah, NJ).

3. This quote was found on page 153 of Liping Ma's book.

CHAPTER 11

1. The term "parrot math" is used by Thomas C. O'Brien in a *Phi Delta Kappan* article entitled "Parrot Math," and published in February 1999 (vol. 80, issue 6, pp. 434–438). In the article, O'Brien accuses those against NCTM of "employ[ing] emotionally loaded labels. (Children's classifying, inferring, generalizing, hypothesizing, and other basic acts of thinking are dubbed 'fuzzy math'; thus I see my use of 'parrot math' as only fair.)" This is found on page 435 of his article. I find it interesting that he complains about name-calling by calling names. Nevertheless, the term "parrot mathematics" is descriptive of what NCTM-oriented supporters think of traditional mathematics.

APPENDIX 1

1. This quote is from "Silence and Policy Talk: Historical Puzzles about Gender and Education," in *Educational Researcher,* authors D. Tyack and E. Hasnot, 1988 (vol. 17, issue 3, pp. 33–41, with the quote found on page 37).

However, I actually took the quote from a source that was also quoting the quote. That source was very helpful in writing this appendix. The source is G. Leder's chapter, "Mathematics and Gender: Changing Perspectives," found on pp. 597–622 in *Handbook of Research on Mathematics Teaching and Learning*, edited by D. A. Grouws, published in 1992 by Simon & Schuster Macmillan, New York.

2. This is from G. Leder's chapter, mentioned in the first note. The page of this quote is 607.

APPENDIX 3

1. See my article with my colleague Ron Regal for more information on placement testing (C. M. Latterell and R. R. Regal. "Are Placement Tests for Incoming Undergraduate Mathematics Students Worth the Expense of Administration?" *PRIMUS* 13(2)(2003): 152–164). By the way, we answer the question—Are placement tests for incoming undergraduate mathematics students worth the expense of administration?—with a "no."

Bibliography

Arem, C. (1993). *Conquering math anxiety: A self-help workbook*. Pacific Grove, CA: Brooks/Cole Publishing Company.

Benacerraf, P., and H. Putnam, eds. (1983). *Philosophy of mathematics*. Cambridge: Cambridge University Press.

Burns, M. (1998). *Math: Facing an American phobia*. Sausalito, CA. Author.

Ernest, P. (1991). *Philosophy of mathematics education*. Bristol, PA: Falmer Press.

Grouws, D., ed. (1992). *Handbook of research on mathematics teaching and learning*. New York: Simon & Schuster Macmillan.

Kilpatrick, J. (1997, October). *Five lessons from the New Math era*. Paper presented at the Reflecting on Sputnik: Linking the Past, Present, and Future of Educational Reform Symposium, National Academy of Sciences, Washington, D.C. Retrieved January 23, 2004, from http://www.nas.edu/sputnik/kilpat2.htm.

Klein, D. (2003). A brief history of American K–12 mathematics education in the twentieth century. In J. Royer, ed., *Mathematical Cognition* (chapter 7). Greenwich, CT: Information Age Publishing.

Latterell, C. M. (2000). *Assessing NCTM standards-oriented and traditional students' problem-solving ability using multiple-choice and open-ended questions*. Unpublished doctoral dissertation, University of Iowa.

Latterell, C. M. (2003). Testing the problem-solving skills of students in an NCTM-oriented curriculum. *Mathematics Educator* 13(1): 5–14.

Latterell, C. M. (2004, February). College corner. *MathBits*. Minnesota Council of Teachers of Mathematics.

Latterell, C. M., and L. Copes (2003). Can we reach definitive conclusions in mathematics education research? *Phi Delta Kappan* 85(3): 207–211.

Latterell, C. M., and R. R. Regal (2003). Are placement tests for incoming undergraduate mathematics students worth the expense of administration? *PRIMUS* 13(2): 152–164.

Latterell, C. M., and K. A. Wohlhuter (2004). Beginning secondary mathematics teachers: A snapshot across one state. *FOCUS: On Learning Problems in Mathematics* 26(1): 23–33.

Leder, G. (1992). Mathematics and gender: Changing perspectives. In D. A. Grouws, ed., *Handbook of research on mathematics teaching and learning* (pp. 597–622) New York: Simon & Schuster Macmillan.

Ma, L. (1999). *Knowing and teaching elementary mathematics*. Mahwah, NJ: Lawrence Erlbaum Associates.

National Commission on Excellence in Education (1983). *A nation at risk.* Washington, D.C.: U.S. Government Printing Office.

National Council of Teachers of Mathematics. (1970). *A history of mathematics education in the United States and Canada.* Reston, VA: Author.

National Council of Teachers of Mathematics. (1980). *Agenda for action.* Reston, VA: Author.

National Council of Teachers of Mathematics. (1989). *Curriculum and evaluation standards for school mathematics.* Reston, VA: Author.

National Council of Teachers of Mathematics. (1991). *Professional standards for teaching mathematics.* Reston, VA: Author.

National Council of Teachers of Mathematics. (1995). *Assessment standards for school mathematics.* Reston, VA: Author.

National Council of Teachers of Mathematics. (2000a). *Principles and standards for school mathematics.* Reston, VA: Author.

National Council of Teachers of Mathematics. (2000b). *Answers to frequently asked questions about Principles and standards for school mathematics.* Reston, VA: Author.

O'Brien, T. C. (1999). Parrot math. *Phi Delta Kappan* 80(6): 434–438.

Reyes, R. E. (2000). Doctorates in mathematics education: An acute shortage. *Notices of the American Mathematics Society* 46(10): 1267–1270.

Reyes, R. E., and J. Kilpatrick (2000). *One field, many paths: U.S. doctoral programs in mathematics education.* Washington, D.C.: American Mathematical Society.

Schoen, H. L., and C. R. Hirsch (2003). Responding to calls for change in high school mathematics: Implications for collegiate mathematics. *American Mathematical Monthly* 110: 109–123.

Schoen, H. L., and S. W. Ziebarth (1998). High school mathematics curriculum reform: Rationale, research, and recent developments. In P. S. Hlebowitsh and W. G. Wraga, eds., *Annual review of research for school leaders* (pp. 141–191). New York: Macmillan.

Senk, S., and D. Thompson, eds. (2003). *Standards-based school mathematics curricula*. Mahwah, NJ: Lawrence Erlbaum Associates.

Steffe, L., P. Nesher, P. Cobb, G. Goldin, and B. Greer, eds. (1996). *Theories of mathematical learning*. Mahwah, NJ: Lawrence Erlbaum Associates.

Stevenson, H. W., and J. W. Stigler (1992). *The learning gap*. New York: Simon & Schuster.

Stigler, J. W., and J. Hiebert (1999). *The teaching gap*. New York: Simon & Schuster.

Tyack, D., and E. Hasnot (1988). Silence and policy talk: Historical puzzles about gender and education. *Educational Researcher* 17(3): 33–41.

Wilson, J. L., and C. M. Latterell (2001). Nerds? Or nuts? Pop culture portrayals of mathematicians. *et cetera* 58: 172–178.

Wilson, S. (2003). *California dreaming: Reforming mathematics education*. London: Yale University Press.

Index

ABOUT THE AUTHOR

CARMEN M. LATTERELL, Ph.D., is Assistant Professor of Mathematics at the University of Minnesota, Duluth. She has taught mathematics at all levels since 1988. She is a frequent contributor to research journals on the subject of mathematics education.